...l policy

STUDIES IN THE UK ECONOMY

UK fiscal policy

Susan Grant
West Oxfordshire College, Witney

Series Editor
Bryan Hurl
Head of Economics, Harrow School

Heinemann Educational
a division of Heinemann Publishers (Oxford) Ltd.
Halley Court, Jordan Hill, Oxford OX2 8EJ

OXFORD LONDON EDINBURGH
MADRID ATHENS BOLOGNA PARIS
MELBOURNE SYDNEY AUCKLAND SINGAPORE TOKYO
IBADAN NAIROBI HARARE GABORONE
PORTSMOUTH NH (USA)

First published 1994

98 97 96 95 94
10 9 8 7 6 5 4 3 2 1

British Library Cataloguing in Publication Data

A catalogue record for this book is available from the British Library

ISBN 0 435 33026 8

Typeset and illustrated by Taurus Graphics, Kidlington, Oxon.

Printed and bound in Great Britain by Clays Ltd, St Ives plc

Acknowledgements

The author would like to thank Bryan Hurl, Sue Walton and Alistair Christie for their considerable assistance.

The publishers would like to thank the following for permission to reproduce copyright material: Associated Examing Board for the questions on pp. 6–7, 22, 46–47, 59 and 80; Andrew Britton for the extract in the question on p. 71; Mel Calman for the cartoons on pp. 4, 17, 41 and 79; the Central Statistical Office for the data used in the question on p. 7; the Commision of the European Communities for the chart on p. 64; the Conservative Research Department for the extract in the question in p. 60; Paul Craig Roberts for the article from the *National Westminister Bank Quartely Review* in the question on pp. 46–47; *The Economist* for the extract on p. 84; The Fabian Society for the extract in the question p. 60; the *Financial Times* for the diagram on p. 25; *The Guardian* for the extracts on pp. 13, 20 and 53; Newspaper Publishing plc for the extract from *The Independent* on p. 10, and for the extract on p. 43 and cartoons by Peter Shrank on pp. 27 and 30 from the *Independent on Sunday*; the Institute for Fiscal Studies for the data on p. 15; Northern Examinations and Assessment Board for the questions on pp. 6, 22, 36, 59, 70 and 80; Northern Ireland Schools Examinations and Assessment Council for the questions on pp. 59 and 80; *The Observer* for the article by William Keegan on p. 14; Oxford and Cambridge Schools Examination Board for the questions on pp. 22, 36, 60–61, 70 and 71–72; Chris Riddell for the cartoons on pp. 18, 21 and 68; © Times Newspapers Ltd 1992/3 for the cartoon by Ken Pyne on p. 74 and the cartoon by Richard Willson p. 83, both originally published in *The Times*; University of Cambridge Local Examinations Syndicate for the questions on pp. 22, 23–24 and 46; University of London Examinations and Assessment Council for the questions on pp. 6, 22, 35, 46, 59, 70–71 and 81; University of Oxford Delegacy of Local Examinations for the questions on pp. 36 and 46; Welsh Joint Education Committee for the questions on pp. 6 and 46; Margaret Wilkinson for the diagram on p. 57.

The publishers have made every effort to contact the correct copyright holders. However, if any material has been incorrectly acknowledged, the publishers would be pleased to make the necessary arrangements at the earliest opportunity.

Contents

Preface

In the 1980s, fiscal policy was downgraded to a supply-side role and had to play handmaiden to pre-eminent monetary policy. Now, in the 1990s, with a burgeoning public sector borrowing requirement, with a structural as well as cyclical imbalance, it is back in the forefront of policy action.

The two fiscally deflationary budgets of 1993 set the government on the defensive when it was striving for growth out of the 1990–92 recession. If the Chancellor of the Exchequer is reduced to dismissing unpleasant fiscal facts as 'piffle' then fiscal policy has clearly returned to centre stage.

Susan Grant is an experienced teacher, examiner and regular contributor to *British Economy Survey*, fully capable of covering this subject to the level A level students will appreciate.

Bryan Hurl
Series Editor

Introduction

There are many possible instruments of fiscal policy. However, fiscal policy can actually be defined quite simply. It includes:

any measure which alters taxation and/or public expenditure in terms of amount, composition or timing.

So, for example, a government decision to build a road a year later than originally planned is a fiscal policy measure.

Fiscal policy affects the lives of people in many ways. For instance it can influence what goods are produced and bought, how many hours people work, what goods are imported and the rate of inflation.

From approximately 1940 to 1979 fiscal policy was used principally to influence aggregate demand. However, most economists now recognize that changes in taxes and public spending can be used as instruments of both demand side and supply side economic management.

Chapter 1 examines the reasons for having a fiscal policy. Governments intervene in the economy to correct *market* failure but in doing so risk encountering *government* failure. Both these areas are discussed. The more specific aims of fiscal policy are then outlined and a brief history of fiscal policy is given.

In Chapter 2 a number of aspects of taxation and public expenditure are discussed. The types of taxes are described and the aims of taxation, touched on in Chapter 1, are explored in more detail. Not all taxes are viewed as bad and the benefits conferred by Pigouvian and 'green' taxes are discussed. Consideration is also given to the argument advanced by an increasing number of economists that tax expenditures (revenue not collected from taxation) should be reduced. Fiscal neutrality aims to avoid distorting the behaviour of economic agents by removing differences in the tax treatment of people and firms undertaking the same activities. Reducing tax expenditures would change the tax burden. The other arm of fiscal policy is government expenditure. The different categories are described and then some of the many reasons for the rise in public expenditure in the twentieth century are explored. One form of public expenditure which is declining in the UK is spending on defence and the implications of the peace dividend are discussed. The chapter concludes by looking at how public expenditure is planned.

Chapter 3 is about the relationship between government expenditure and taxation. It distinguishes between reflationary and deflationary fiscal policy and makes clear the difference between a structural and a cyclical budget deficit. PSBR and PSDR are defined and their significance discussed. How a PSBR can be financed is discussed at some length. A public sector borrowing requirement arises from public sector expenditure exceeding revenue and adds to the national debt. How significant an impact the national debt has on the economy is discussed.

The conduct of fiscal policy is explored in Chapter 4. Stabilization policies, automatic stabilizers, demand management and fine tuning are explained. A comparison of rules and discretionary fiscal policy is made and the medium-term financial strategy and a balanced budget strategy are discussed.

In Chapter 5 two major current issues in fiscal policy are explored. The first is whether an increase in public expenditure increases private sector expenditure, reduces it or merely replaces it. This is referred to as the 'crowding out' debate. The second issue is how our present tax system could be reformed. This involves an examination of the effects of changing income tax rates, tax avoidance and evasion, switching reliance from direct to indirect taxation, 'sin' taxes, income redistribution and the 'poverty trap'.

Chapter 6 is about how membership of the European Union is affecting UK fiscal policy and how it is likely to do so in the future. The UK's contribution to the EU's budget is explained and the effect that the movement towards greater European integration, including the harmonization of taxes, is having on the economy are discussed.

Chapter 7 concentrates on local government spending and revenue. The chapter considers whether local taxation should be based on the ability to pay and /or the benefit principle, and the three main possible ways of raising finance – a local sales tax, a local income tax, and a property tax. Then recent sources of local authority finance, including the current council tax, are explored .

The final chapter looks at the problems and the future of fiscal policy. Although there are a number of potential difficulties involved – including time lags, political cycles, pressure groups and policy conflicts – the central argument advanced is that fiscal policy is likely to become more important and significant in the future.

Chapter One

The nature of fiscal policy

*'No government activity touches more pockets than fiscal policy,
whether in the field of taxation or public expenditure.'*   Keith Marder

Market failure

A government raises taxes and spends money to correct **market failure.**
Left to free market forces an economy may not produce the quantity of
goods and services that people want at the prices that reflect their marginal utilities. This failure to achieve the optimum allocation of
resources arises from:

- a lack of financial incentive to produce public goods;
- under- provision of merit goods;
- provision of demerit goods;
- failure to take into account other externalities;
- the short time-span of some entrepreneurs' investment decisions;
- the tendency for imperfect competition to develop in the goods and
  factor markets;
- immobility of some factors of production;
- imperfect information;
- advertising that distorts consumer choice;
- the inability of some (e.g. the young, old or ill) to earn incomes.

Government failure

What degree of **government intervention** economists and politicians
consider necessary is influenced by their normative views on :

- the extent of market failure;
- how effective they believe the government intervention will be on
  correcting it.

Indeed, there is no guarantee that government intervention will always
improve the allocation of resources. Just as information can be lacking
in a free market, so there can be insufficient and /or inaccurate information in the public sector. Information is costly and is difficult to collect –
for instance, it is difficult to attach monetary values to negative and
positive externalities. In a free market, entrepreneurs have a financial

incentive to develop monopolies, which may result in price being higher and output lower than the allocatively efficient levels.

Government failure can also arise from financial self-interest. In this case it may be the self-interest of civil servants. The pay and status of senior civil servants are influenced by the sizes of their departments, which can result in the over-expansion of some government activities. In addition, policy decisions can be influenced by political as well as economic factors. (The problems of fiscal policy are discussed in the final chapter.)

So whilst **fiscal policy** exists to correct market failure, changes in taxes and **public expenditure** may be introduced in order to make the fiscal policy more effective in reducing market failure, or to correct government failure arising from previous fiscal policy decisions. For example, a government may reduce the rate of income tax because it believes private sector demand is too low (market failure) and/or because it considers that the rate is discouraging people from working (government failure).

Aims of fiscal policy

As we have seen, fiscal policy (in common with most other forms of government policy) attempts to offset the shortcomings of the free market system. More specifically, fiscal policy aims to influence:

- *The distribution of income and wealth.* Income tax and state benefits redistribute income from the rich to the poor.
- *The allocation of resources.* Government expenditure, financed by **taxation,** can shift resources from the private to the public sector. There may, for example, be an increase in the taxation on cigarettes and a rise in spending on state health care. This will shift resources from private sector cigarette production to the NHS. Fiscal policy can also influence the allocation of resources in the private sector. Recently taxation has been used to encourage a switch from leaded to unleaded petrol. It can also discriminate in favour of investment by giving firms investment subsidies financed by taxation on consumer spending.
- *The stabilization of the economy.* This is concerned with achieving macro policy objectives, including high employment, growth and price stability.

Obviously a change in taxation and /or government expenditure may be targeted at achieving one specific type of aim but will also influence the other two. For example, a reduction in income tax, implemented to increase aggregate demand, may increase the uneven distribution of income.

A brief history of fiscal policy

The use of fiscal policy has changed through the twentieth century as a result of changes in:

- economic theories being followed;
- economic circumstances;
- the focus of government objectives.

The work of Keynes in the 1930s and 40s led to increased government intervention. Indeed, from the Second World War until the mid–70s, fiscal policy followed an interventionist Keynesian approach. **Demand management** was used mainly in an attempt to achieve full employment. Governments would borrow and spend when private sector demand was low.

After 1975 there was a move away from the active use of fiscal policy, and more reliance was placed on monetary policy. A number of economists questioned the effectiveness of fiscal policy – and indeed of most forms of government policy. They argued that an expansionary fiscal policy, designed to achieve full employment, often does not work; instead, in the long run, it gives rise to inflationary pressure and balance of payments difficulties. These problems cause governments to reduce aggregate demand and give rise to **stop/go cycles.**

Attention in the 1970s and 80s also shifted from full employment to price stability as the prime objective. Greater emphasis was placed on the supply side of the economy, and most of the tax changes implemented in the 1980s were designed to increase incentives for workers and entrepreneurs. Recently as the UK has approached, albeit hesitantly, greater EU integration, it has been debated whether in the future the UK will be able to operate an independent fiscal policy. However, the recession of the early 1990s and changes in government views and priorities have witnessed signs of a return to a more active fiscal policy.

Whatever changes are made to the fiscal policy in the future, it will continue to have a significant impact on people's lives. As Keith Marder has indicated, our living standards are affected by the taxes we pay and the benefits we receive from government expenditure.

```
┌─────────────────────────────────────────────────────┐
│                    KEY WORDS                          │
│                                                       │
│   Market failure              Taxation                │
│   Government intervention     Stabilization           │
│   Government failure          Demand management       │
│   Fiscal policy               Stop/go cycles          │
│   Public expenditure                                  │
└─────────────────────────────────────────────────────┘
```

Reading list

Beardshaw, J., Chapter 41 in *Economics: A Student's Guide*, 3rd edn, Pitman, 1992.

N.I.E.S.R., Chapters 4 and 7 in *The UK Economy*, 2nd edn, Heinemann Educational, 1993.

Maunder, P., et al., Chapter 31 in *Economics Explained*, 2nd edn, Collins Educational, 1991.

Wilkinson, M., Chapter 2 in *Equity and Efficiency*, Heinemann Educational, 1993.

Essay topics

1. What do you understand by the term 'standard of living' ? How can it be measured? To what extent, if any, have recent changes in the government's taxation policies affected the standard of living of UK households? (Joint Matriculation Board, A/S level, 1992)

2. Examine the macro economic implications of a substantial increase in public expenditure on a national road building programme. (University of London Examinations and Assessment Council, 1991)

3. (a) Why has it been argued that fiscal policy might act as an instrument for managing aggregate demand in the economy? (b) Why has it been argued that fiscal policy of this sort: (i) might be ineffective; (ii) might be effective in principle but cannot be operated successfully in practice? (Welsh Joint Education Committee, 1990)

Data Response Question 1

Taxation and social security contributions

This task is based on a question set by the Associated Examining Board in 1991. Study Tables A and B and answer the questions that follow.

Table A shows taxation and social security contributions as a percentage of national income. Table B shows the revenue raised from the different categories of taxation as a percentage of total revenue raised by taxes and social security contributions. (Taxes on capital are *not* included, but these account for only a small proportion of total taxation in any year.)

Table A

	1976	1981	1986
Total taxes and social security contributions as a percentage of GNP at factor cost	39%	43%	44%

Table B

	1976	1981	1986
Direct taxes on households	39%	30%	28%
Direct taxes on corporate incomes	5%	9%	11%
Indirect taxes	36%	43%	43%
Social security contributions	19%	17%	18%

1. (i) What do the data suggest happened to the overall burden of taxation in the UK between 1976 and 1986? Justify your answer.
   (ii) Suggest and explain **two** possible causes of the change you have described.
2. Describe the main changes in the pattern of taxation which took place between 1976 and 1986.
3. Discuss the likely effects of the changes you described in question 2 on: (i) the distribution of household incomes; (ii) the incentive to effort and enterprise.

Chapter Two

Taxation and public expenditure

'There is no such thing as a good tax.'   Winston Churchill

The structure of taxation

Taxation is a controversial subject. Disagreements exist about the aims of taxation, the qualities of a 'good' tax, and the effects of taxation.

A government has to decide on its **tax base** (i.e. the coverage of what is taxed). For instance, the tax base of VAT includes cars but not books. The government also has to decide on the incidence of tax. This refers to the distribution of the burden of the tax. The **formal incidence** of the tax falls on those who have the legal liability to pay, but the **effective incidence** refers to those who are less well off as a result of the tax.

Types of taxes

Taxes can be categorized in a number of ways. They can be divided into:

- **Taxes on income** (e.g. income tax and corporation tax).
- **Taxes on expenditure** (e.g. VAT and excise duties).
- **Taxes on wealth** (e.g. capital gains and inheritance tax).
- **Direct and indirect taxes.** Direct taxes, which are collected by the Inland Revenue, are taxes on income and wealth. As their incidence cannot be shifted, the burden is borne by those upon whom the taxes are levied. Indirect taxes are collected by the Customs and Excise Department and, in the case of vehicle excise duty, by the Department of Transport. They are taxes on expenditure, and so the burden of an indirect tax may be passed on – in whole or in part – to others by means of higher prices.
- **Progressive, proportional and regressive taxes.** A progressive tax takes a higher percentage of an income as that income rises. A **proportional tax** takes a fixed percentage. A **regressive tax** takes a smaller percentage of an income as that income rises, and so this tax takes proportionately more from the lower-paid. (See Figure 1).

Aims of taxation

Many people believe that the main aim of taxation is to raise revenue. However, a government could finance its expenditure by borrowing or

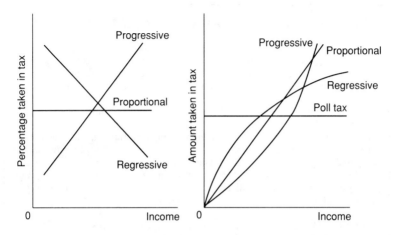

Figure 1 Types of taxes

by printing money. The reason it does not raise most of its money in this way is that it would add too much to private sector demand and would be inflationary. *The main aim of taxation is not to raise revenue but to reduce private sector demand, thereby releasing resources for use by the public sector in a non-inflationary way.*

So taxes are used to influence the allocation of resources and (as we have seen in Chapter 1) income distribution and stabilization of the economy. More specifically, taxes may be used to:

- discourage the consumption of demerit goods;
- reduce income and wealth inequalities;
- discourage the purchase of imports;
- influence the level of aggregate demand;
- influence the level of aggregate supply.

How National Insurance contributions (NICs) differ from other taxes

NICs are compulsory payments by both employers and employees to the national insurance fund, based on each individual's pay. They are not collected by the taxation departments. Unlike other taxes, they give rise to benefits to the employee in the form of entitlement to future benefit payments in the event of sickness, unemployment or eventually old age. As there is an upper limit to NIC contributions, this is a regressive tax.

Why not put a tax on antisocial behaviour?

HAMISH McRAE

If we want to discourage lager louts we should increase the tax on lager. If the Government were serious about improving the national diet it could consider a tax on fatty foods; we already pay VAT on chocolate digestives (which count as confectionery) and not on the regular sort. We could use differential VAT rates to charge more for pornographic magazines than for learned journals, more for violent films than for family entertainment. The body count in some of Shakespeare's plays could mean that he hit the top VAT rate – it could be done, though, if society thought it important.

But it is the positive use of the tax mechanism that will always attract most attention. If we want to encourage adult education and training, why not allow such costs against personal taxation? If we believe that families which stick together are more likely to bring up healthy, balanced children, there should be tax incentives in favour of cohabitation. If we want to rebuild marriage as an institution, maybe the tax net should be still further biased towards it. If we want to encourage preventative health care, then introduce allowances for annual check-ups.

Source: *The Independent*, 10 March 1993

Qualities of a good tax

Adam Smith put forward four principles of taxation. These were:

- *Equity* – the amount of tax people pay should be based on their ability to pay.
- *Certainty* – the amount of tax to be paid, when it is to be paid and how it is to be paid should be known.
- *Convenience* – the tax should be easy to understand, to pay and to collect.
- *Economy* – the cost of collection and administration should be small relative to the tax revenue for the payer and the government. For firms there are **compliance costs** of understanding the frequently changing tax law, training employees, maintaining records, calculating taxes due and making tax returns and payments.

Since Adam Smith's day, the quality of equity has been developed and extra qualities of a good tax have been defined: economists now distinguish between horizontal and vertical equity. **Horizontal equity** occurs when people in the same financial circumstances pay the same amount of tax. In practice this may not work if some people evade tax or if they hire specialist advice to reduce their payments legally. **Vertical equity** exists when people earning higher incomes pay more tax.

The qualities of *flexibility* and *efficiency* are also now thought to be desirable. A tax which can be changed easily, or which changes automatically, to achieve government aims is advantageous.

Pigouvian taxes

A tax which improves economic efficiency is regarded as being beneficial and so contradicts Winston Churchill's view that there cannot be a good tax. Efficiency can be increased by a **Pigouvian tax**. This is a tax designed with the prime aim not of raising revenue but of correcting an externality. It seeks to increase welfare by equating **marginal social benefit** and **marginal social cost**. Where the private costs of an activity do not cover its full social costs, and hence there are negative externalities, output will be higher than the socially optimum level. A government can seek to remedy this situation by imposing a tax on the activity equal to the gap between marginal social cost and marginal private cost (XZ in Figure 2).

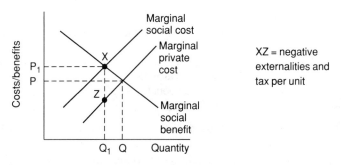

XZ = negative externalities and tax per unit

Figure 2 Correcting a negative externality

Tax expenditure

Tax expenditure is the name given to revenue that is *not collected* by means of taxation, because of tax relief, concessions and privileges. This can be used as a substitute for direct government spending. Examples of tax expenditure are tax relief on mortgage interest, pension contributions, and personal equity plans (PEPs).

Tax expenditures are, however, controversial, for the following reasons:

- They are not recorded in government spending totals, and so do not come under the same scrutiny as direct forms of public expenditure.
- The sums involved are large, they considerably reduce potential tax revenues and they give significant benefit to the recipients. Indeed if tax expenditures were reduced, government spending could be increased and/or taxes could be cut.
- Once incorporated in a tax system they tend to stay even when their original purpose has disappeared.

GREEN TAXES

Green taxes are examples of Pigouvian taxes. They are used to improve the environment by reducing negative externalities, including traffic congestion, water pollution and the greenhouse effect. Green taxes have a number of advantages, including:

- internalising negative externalities, thereby turning them into private costs;
- providing an incentive for firms to engage in a continuous search to reduces these costs;
- raising revenue;
- possibly making consumers more aware of the environmental effects of the products.

However, green taxes have a number of possible disadvantages:

- they are likely to be inflationary, in the short run;
- if other countries do not impose them it reduces this country's competitiveness;
- they are likely to place a greater burden on the poor than on the rich, because most indirect taxes are regressive;
- it is difficult to judge the appropriate rate of tax.

It is possible that tax expenditures can serve a social purpose – for instance, the tax relief from income tax on low incomes. However, whilst some may have been designed to help the poor, in practice most benefit the rich (who are more likely to own houses and have personal equity plans) and particular interest groups at the expense of others, thereby distorting economic behaviour.

Fiscal neutrality

In the 1970s, attention on taxation largely moved from its effects on aggregate demand to its effects on aggregate supply through its impact on the number of hours people work and how much firms invest and produce. One feature of this new focus was concern with promoting **fiscal neutrality**. Fiscal neutrality seeks to raise tax revenue in a way which does not distort the behaviour of firms and households unless this is the deliberate intention of the government. (For instance, a government may raise the tax on cigarettes specifically to discourage smoking.) A neutral tax is one which leaves households and firms making the same decision whether they look at their income before or after tax. In practice, of course, all taxes are likely to alter the behaviour of people, but *what the idea of a neutral tax emphasizes is that tax should avoid unintended and harmful changes in behaviour.* Nevertheless it is important to consider the overall impact of the tax and benefit system. A particular tax may be regressive or have other undesirable features but may be offset by other taxes.

We obviously do not have fiscal neutrality in the UK. Should we seek it? Many economists believe that we should eliminate, or at least reduce, some of the unfairness and inconsistencies that are contained in our tax system, particularly in relation to savings and investment. Removing or reducing some tax privileges gained by special interest groups should increase equity and efficiency, simplify the tax system and remove distortions. In addition, inefficiency arising from individuals and firms acting to reduce their tax burden will fall. All forms of tax privilege cause actual tax rates to be higher than would be required under a fiscally neutral system.

If it is thought that greater fiscal neutrality would be beneficial, it could be achieved in one of two main ways. One is by **levelling down** (i.e. removing existing tax privileges). The other is by **levelling up** (extending tax privileges).

In practice it is difficult to establish the benchmark against which a tax system should be judged. There are differences of opinion as to what constitutes a neutral tax system. Some economists interpret it to mean one in which the government intervenes to a considerable extent to offset existing externalities.

The tax burden

The **tax burden** is the total amount of money people and firms pay in tax, and is often expressed as a percentage of gross domestic product

---

At the hands of the tax collector

In Britain today people pay a vast array of taxes. Most of the money raised is used to pay for the services provided by national and local government – including the police, the National Health Service, the state education system and retirement pensions. Since 1973 some of these taxes have also helped to fund the activities of the European Community.

All governments need to raise taxes in order to perform their roles. In Britain the Inland Revenue is responsible for assessing and collecting taxes. The increase in the burden faced by taxpayers during the 20th century reflects not only the cost of fighting two world wars, but the extension of state power into new areas.

In the year before the 1890 Budget, when David Lloyd George (1863–1945) who was Chancellor, first proposed retirement pensions, the Inland Revenue raised £96 million in taxes. This year it will raise £80,000,000,000.

Source: *The Guardian,* 25 Feb. 1992

(GDP). Most people believe that the tax burden in the UK is high. In fact the UK is a middle-ranked country, with its tax burden below many advanced countries, including Sweden, Norway and France. Most advanced countries in the 1980s reduced reliance on income tax and placed more reliance on indirect taxes. The overall tax burden was not reduced but the distribution of the tax burden changed, moving from the rich to the poor. The two budgets held in 1993 saw a rise in the overall tax burden in the UK.

Revealed: The Chancellor's real tax rise

The combined effect of the 1993 Budgets is to raise taxes by between £15bn and £17bn over a three-year period, equivalent to 10 pence on the basic rate of income tax. This is sensational stuff.

WILLIAM KEEGAN

In the old days at the *Financial Times*, we had a custom whereby it was open to people to write articles on the lines of 'Second Thoughts on the Budget'. Sometimes such articles bore only a tenuous relation to the interpretation put upon the Budget the previous day by the same author; occasionally they involved a complete change of mind.

I have to say that there has been no change of mind on my own part in the past week: indeed, there has, if anything, been a hardening of attitude – a process which has been assisted by attendance at the various hearings of the Treasury Select Committee, where Treasury and Bank of England officials have been dotting the i's and crossing the t's of the Budget.

The most important aspect of the Budget, skilfully underplayed by the Chancellor in his speech, is the size of the tax increases. The combined effect of the 1993 Lamont/Clarke Budgets is to raise the annual tax take by between £15 billion and £17 billion over a three-year period, equivalent to a 10 pence rise in the basic rate of income tax.

This is sensational stuff, and it was no wonder that the Chancellor wished to divert attention by drawing attention to a £3.5 billion reduction in public spending plans.

In meetings abroad with his finance minister colleagues, Clarke will now be able to boast about the degree to which the British Government is grasping the nettle of the fiscal problems which are allegedly afflicting governments throughout the western world.

But it is doubtful whether, at home, he will spend much time illustrating the severity of the budget by saying it is the equivalent of a 10 per cent rise in the basic rate of income tax.

The UK's fiscal problem was of the Government's own making, in that during the 1980s it behaved as though North Sea revenues would stay at the same level for ever, and the outrageous tax cuts of 1988 would somehow finance themselves. If Labour had won the election of 1992, it would have had a very hard time convincing the electorate that tax increases were necessary; indeed, it had enough trouble with its ill-conceived mix of tax increases for some and reductions for others. As Neil Kinnock told an audience at the Institute of Historical Research last week, it was 'the cumulative effect of the Tory Tax Bomb campaign' which did for Labour, as '[the don't knows] made up their minds to play what they thought was a safe game'.

Source: *Observer,* 12 December 1993

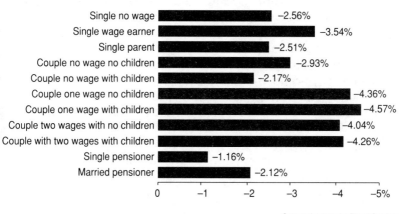

Source: Institute for Fiscal Studies

Figure 3 Effects on household income of the two budgets in 1993 (percentage of post-tax income)

The amount of tax which is paid can be influenced by fiscal drag and by fiscal dividend. **Fiscal drag** occurs when rises in money incomes drag people into higher tax brackets, causing their post-tax real incomes to fall. However, the Rooker–Wise clause provides that tax allowances be raised in line with inflation unless the budget specifically provides otherwise. **Fiscal dividend** relates to the fact that, as the economy grows, extra tax income becomes available to the Treasury without increasing tax rates.

Forms of public expenditure
As with taxation, public expenditure can be classified in a number of different ways. It can be divided into:

- *Central and local government spending.* Central government expenditure accounts for about three-quarters of all public spending, and local government for the remaining one-quarter.
- *Capital and current expenditure and transfer payments.* **Capital expenditure** is spending on investment. This comes in a variety of forms. Spending on the construction of schools and other forms of social capital contributes to economic growth by increasing the quality of the workforce. Investment in infrastructure such as transport adds directly to output and increases the efficiency of the private sector. **Current expenditure** on goods and services is incurred in meeting the day to day running costs of services, including the

salaries of public employees. **Transfer payments** include the whole range of social security benefits, housing subsidies, students' grants, financial aid to industry and agriculture and interest on the national debt.

- *Exhaustive and non-exhaustive expenditure.* Whereas capital and current spending are classified as **exhaustive** or **final expenditure,** transfer payments are classified as **non-exhaustive expenditure.** This is because the capital and current spending use resources which could have been used in the private sector, whereas transfer payments do not directly absorb resources. What they do is to redistribute spending power to pensioners and other recipients of state aid. The effect is to reallocate private claims on output, generally in favour of low-income groups, without actually drawing resources into the public sector.

Final expenditure adds directly to GDP whereas transfer payments do not.

By far the largest component of public expenditure is the social security budget. In 1993, 27 per cent of total government expenditure was for social security, 12 per cent for health and $9\frac{1}{2}$ per cent for defence.

The measure of public expenditure which is used for the formulation of macroeconomic policy is **general government expenditure** (Figure 4). This includes central government and local government spending and interest payable on the national debt. It is, therefore, essentially

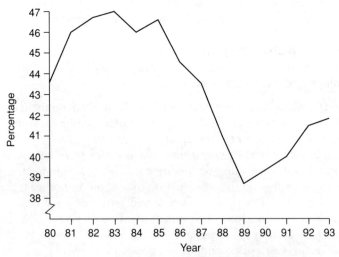

Figure 4 Real GGE as a percentage of real GDP

total public spending and represents the amount which needs to be raised by taxation and/or borrowing.

Influences on the level of public expenditure

Public expenditure in the UK and other advanced countries has increased significantly during the twentieth century. There are many reasons for this:

- Much of public expenditure depends on demand influences and many state-provided services are **income elastic**. For example, as incomes rise a higher proportion of young people want to enter higher education.
- Minimum standards rise over time, and this leads to a rise in the transfer budget with state benefits increasing.
- In a developed economy the enjoyment of private goods requires complementary **public goods**. For example, to enjoy a car requires public sector outlay on roads.
- Many government services are labour-intensive. So rises in wages have a significant impact on the cost of providing the services.
- As people live longer and as advances take place in medical knowledge, health care costs rise. The proportion and numbers of elderly people in the population are increasing quite significantly. Government policy at the moment is to reduce the state's long-term commitments to the elderly, by shifting the provisions of pensions and health care and other forms of social services from the public to the private sector.

- Public capital expenditure is also influenced by the stage of economic development. Some economists believe that, at an early stage, high expenditure is required to provide the social and economic infrastructure. Then, in a middle stage of development, less public investment is needed. However, they regard the UK as being in the later stage. This is when old facilities wear out (e.g. bridges and sewers), and when high-quality provision of public facilities (e.g. hospitals) are required.
- Technological change also requires increased government expenditure. It is needed in the development of publicly provided goods like military weapons

and hospital equipment. This tends to generate further spending as the more sophisticated equipment is usually more expensive. Government expenditure may also be needed to develop private sector goods. This is because private sector companies tend to take a short-term view and under-invest in long-term projects.

- Peacock and Wiseman have advanced a 'displacement theory'. They argue that the size of public expenditure is largely determined by the willingness of the electorate to pay taxes, and that public spending is forced up by particular events. During national emergencies, particularly wars, this willingness to pay taxes increases. Wars also focus attention on social problems such as poor health and education standards, which may require government action. People and the government get used to the higher levels, and once a war is over government spending and taxation do not go back to their previous levels.

- Some economists believe that public expenditure is likely to grow more rapidly under a Labour than a Conservative government, on the basis that the former will be more interventionalist and more committed to the public sector. This has not always proved to be the case, but if one government does raise public expenditure this is likely to make it difficult for following administrations to return it to its previous level.

- A **ratchet effect** also results from the business cycle. During booms, public spending is easier to finance owing to buoyant tax revenues (fiscal dividend), and long-term commitments tend to be taken on.
- As society becomes more complex, a new set of remedial public services may be needed such as monopoly controls, traffic controls and pollution controls. Also new policies, such as the council tax, cost money to introduce.
- Pressure groups encourage the government to spend more to benefit their groups. The government itself is likely to want to increase its spending as it approaches a general election in order to increase its popularity.
- Rising crime levels have increased expenditure on law and order.

THE PEACE DIVIDEND

The **peace dividend** refers to the benefits which a country can gain from lower defence expenditure. The movement from A to B on the production possibility curve will occur if resources are moved from producing defence goods to producing civilian goods. The increase in output of civilian goods (e.g. CDs and clothes) is likely to raise living standards.

However, if defence production declines with no corresponding rise in civilian output, unemployment will rise. This situation is shown by the movement from A to C, a point inside the curve.

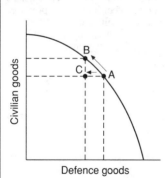

Falling expenditure is likely to reduce output and employment not only in the armed services and the military equipment industries but also in ancillary industries, including those producing uniforms. With a smaller domestic manufacturing base, exports may decline.

UK firms currently account for 20 per cent of the world market in defence exports. Defence spending in the UK will have dropped by about 12 per cent in real terms between 1990/91 and 1995/96, representing about 3.2 per cent of GDP. However, the UK's defence programme will remain one of the highest in Europe.

Planning public expenditure

Under the old system, provisional three-year spending plans were announced each autumn and there was bargaining between individual government departments and the Treasury, with ministers making spending bids. The targets were almost always revised upwards.

The present system, introduced in 1994, called the 'new control total' by the Treasury, seeks to impose discipline on spending ministers. It is a top-down approach which focuses on the allocation of available resources. The total amount to be spent is decided by the cabinet early in each year's public spending round. Then the chief secretary to the Treasury discusses the allocation with departmental ministers. It is possible for ministers to argue over their department's share but not over the total. So any increase in one department's spending means cuts for another department. A committee, chaired by the Chancellor of the Exchequer, decides on the final share-out. The total excludes privatization proceeds, debt interest and social security payments related to unemployment. However, a fall in economic activity does put upward pressure on the control total as it includes items such as housing and incapacity benefits which tend to rise when earnings fall. Also, other demand-led benefits such as retirement pensions and child benefit come within the control total.

TREASURY TARGETS UNIVERSAL BENEFITS

STEPHEN BATES

The Government refused to back down over the possibility of extending prescription charges for children and pensioners yesterday, as it became clear that the bedrock welfare state principle of universal benefits will come under scrutiny in this summer's public expenditure negotiations.

The row presages months of bitter departmental conflicts with the Treasury during what the Chief Secretary to the Treasury, Michael Portillo, has promised will be one of the toughest spending rounds for many years.

Source: *The Guardian*, 21 May 1993

Reducing expenditure

A high level of public expenditure may be a cause for concern for two main and related reasons:

- How is it to be financed?
- Will it encourage or discourage private sector activity?

At present the government's stated objective is to hold the rate of growth of public expenditure below the growth of the economy in the medium term, thus reducing public spending as a proportion of GDP. However, it has been argued that the cyclical nature of employment and other items makes the GGE:GDP ratio an unsatisfactory rule to try to follow. Other economists argue that public expenditure should be determined on the basis of need rather than by following a rule.

KEY WORDS

Tax base
Formal (tax) incidence
Effective (tax) incidence
Taxes on income
Taxes on expenditure
Taxes on wealth
Direct taxes
Indirect taxes
Progressive taxes
Proportional taxes
Regressive taxes
National Insurance
   contributions
Compliance costs
Horizontal equity
Vertical equity
Pigouvian tax
Marginal social benefit
Marginal social cost

Green taxes
Tax expenditure
Fiscal neutrality
Levelling down
Levelling up
Tax burden
Fiscal drag
Fiscal dividend
Capital expenditure
Current expenditure
Transfer payments
Exhaustive (final) expenditure
Non-exhaustive expenditure
General government expenditure
Income elastic
Public goods
Displacement theory
Ratchet effect
Peace dividend

Reading list

Burningham, D., and Davis, J., *Green Economics*, Heinemann Educational, 1994.

Griffiths, A., and Wall, S., Chapters 13 and 14 in *Applied Economics,* Longman, 1993.

N.I.E.S.R., Chapters 3 and 4 in *The UK Economy*, 2nd edn, Heinemann Educational, 1993.

Wilkinson, M., Chapter 7 in *Equity and Efficiency*, Heinemann Educational, 1993.

Whynes, D., Chapter 2 in *Welfare State Economics*, Heinemann Educational, 1992.

Essay topics

1. (a) Distinguish between income and wealth. (b) Discuss the possible economic effects of policies aimed at significantly reducing inequalities in income and wealth. (Associated Examining Board, 1991)
2. 'There are two microeconomic criteria by which to assess tax, efficiency and equity'. With reference to these criteria, examine the effects of (a) a reduction of the higher income tax rate; and (b) an increase in the duty payable on cigarettes (Joint Matriculation Board, A/S level, 1990)
3. 'Between 1979 and 1993 the UK tax system became less progressive'. Explain this statement, using relevant examples. Analyse the possible effects of these changes. (University of London Examinations and Assessment Council, 1993)
4. 'The Conservative Government's consistent aim has been to bring down the tax burden when it is prudent to do so, and in particular, to reduce the basic rate of income tax. Progress has been considerable.' (Conservative Party Campaign Guide, April 1991). Discuss. (Oxford & Cambridge Schools Examination Board, 1992)
5. (a) Using examples, distinguish between direct and indirect taxation. (b) Consider the relative merit of the two forms of taxation. (University of Cambridge Local Examinations Syndicate, 1991)
6. (a) With reference to public expenditure, distinguish between current expenditure, capital expenditure and transfer expenditure. (b) What factors may explain changes in (i) the total level, and (ii) the composition of public expenditure over time? (c) Examine the problems involved in attempting to control public expenditure. (University of London Examinations and Assessment Council, 1993)

Data Response Question 2

The Chancellor's options

This task is based on a question set by the University of Cambridge Local Examinations Syndicate in 1991. The theme is to decide whether the Chancellor should aim to drive down the PSBR or to reduce certain taxes.

Figure A shows that a fall in the public sector borrowing requirement in the period under consideration has been accompanied by a sharp fall in the rate of inflation. Figure B shows that the total tax taken from a married man was still higher in 1985/86 than it was in 1978/79. Study these two charts, and Table A, before answering the questions that follow.

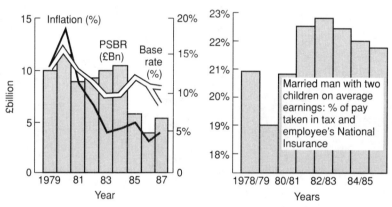

Figure A

Figure B

Table A		GDP change (%)	Inflation change (%)	Consumer spending change (£million)	Investment change (£million)
Option 1 Projected effect of cut of 2p in standard rate of income tax	Year 1	+0.2	0.0	+500	+65
	Year 2	+0.3	+0.3	+815	+100
Option 2 Projected effect of cut in rate of interest by 2%	Year 1	+0.2	−0.4	+580	+215
	Year 2	+0.4	−0.6	+880	+650

1. What indication is there in Figure B that the data relate to direct taxes?
2. With reference to Figure B, explain what is meant by 'the burden of tax'. Describe what has happened to the real burden of direct taxation after 1979.
3. Describe the correlations shown in Figure A. Use economic analysis to explain these relationships.
4. First describe the correlations between projected consumption and investment expenditure shown in Table A, and then explain them.
5. Which of the options – lower taxes or lower interest rates – would you choose? Justify your choice.

Chapter Three
The budget: its economic importance

'An unbalanced budget has been blamed for almost all the ills of human kind except fallen arches.'   B. Guy Peters

The budget

Before the publication of Keynes's *General Theory of Employment, Interest and Money*, the conventional wisdom was that the government should attempt to balance its budget in all circumstances. This was sometimes referred to as 'good housekeeping'.

What Keynes proposed was that the budget position should alter to influence economic activity. Hence, during times of high unemployment the government should implement **reflationary fiscal policy**. This involves the government increasing aggregate demand, which may be achieved by the government spending more than it raises in tax revenue (a **budget deficit**).

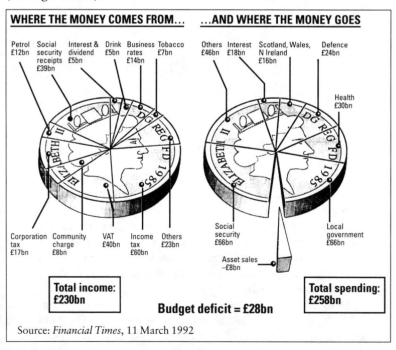

Source: *Financial Times*, 11 March 1992

On the other hand, if private sector demand is thought to be too high and giving rise to inflation and/or a balance of payments deficit, there should be a **deflationary fiscal policy**. This involves reducing aggregate demand and may involve the government raising more in tax revenue than it spends (a **budget surplus**).

Keynesians see the prime objective of the budget as trying to match aggregate demand in the country with the country's potential aggregate supply at the full-employment level. The conventional 45° line in Figure 5 shows the equilibrium of national income (Y) initially being below the full-employment level. The government responds by raising its expenditure from G to G_1, thereby raising national income to the full-employment level at Y_{FE}.

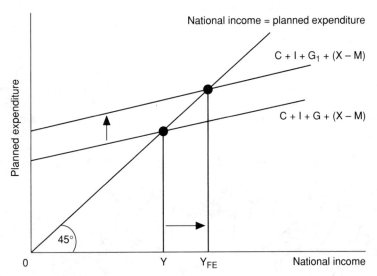

Figure 5 The effect of increased government spending

In the 1970s the Keynesian view of the role of the budget position began to be questioned at governmental level. This is discussed in more detail in Chapter 4.

Nowadays the Chancellor receives advice in preparing his budget from a variety of sources, including the departments of the Inland Revenue and Customs and Excise, the Bank of England, the Treasury and a group of independent economists, dubbed the 'seven wise men' by the media (see page 83).

Since 1993, the budget has been published in November/December. It now includes spending plans as well as taxation decisions. This is in line with the practice followed in most other industrialized countries.

Measuring fiscal stance

The budget position may give a misleading impression of government policy, unless care is taken to interpret it. A budget deficit may be the result of deliberate government policy or may arise through changes in the level of economic activity.

That part of a budget deficit which arises from a planned change in the structure of taxes and/or government spending is known as the **structural deficit.** The part which has been influenced by changes in the level of economic activity is known as the **cyclical deficit.**

Also, it may be difficult to assess what type of government policy is being followed. For instance, a fall in the tax yield and a rise in government spending may be the outcome of a contractionary rather than an expansionary policy. This is because a government seeking to reduce demand may introduce policies which lead to higher unemployment. If this is the case, less income tax, corporation tax and VAT will be paid and the government will have to spend more on unemployment benefit (to be known as **job seekers' allowance** from 1996) and other benefits.

One way of measuring the effect of the budget on the economy which attempts to abstract from cyclical changes is the **full-employment (FE) budget concept.** This involves not measuring the actual government deficit or surplus, which depends on the actual level of income, but

27

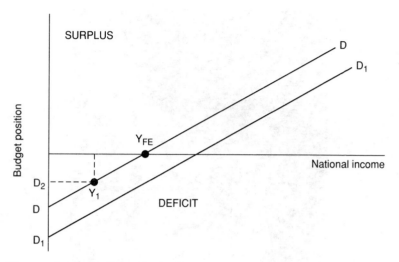

Figure 6 The full employment budget concept

instead the value of the deficit or surplus that would prevail at full employment. In Figure 6, the budget deficit function DD shows no structural deficit, because when the economy is operating at full capacity, expenditure just balances revenue. However, this does not mean that a deficit will never occur. For instance, in a recession income may fall to Y_1 and there will be a deficit of D_2. If the budget deficit function is shown by D_1D_1, then even if output is at its full-employment level, a budget deficit will occur, and this will be a structural deficit.

The full-employment budget position can also be used to compare policies. If one policy would result in a larger surplus than another it would be more contractionary. The reverse is also true, and Figure 6 shows that D_1D_1 is more expansionary than DD.

The public sector current financial position

The **public sector current financial position** is the difference between the total income and the total expenditure of the public sector. It is calculated from:

- the government's budget position;
- local authorities' budget positions;
- the net trading surplus or loss of nationalised industries and public corporations.

The largest component is the government's budget position. A **public sector borrowing requirement (PSBR)** arises when the public sector

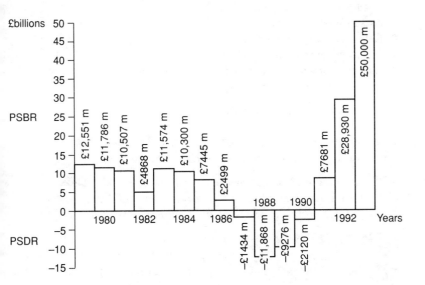

Figure 7 The public sector current financial position 1979–1993

spends more than it raises in revenue. **A public sector debt repayment (PSDR)** occurs when public sector revenue exceeds public sector expenditure.

As indicated above, the actual public sector position can vary from the intended position. For instance, a government may be aiming for a positive PSBR, but if the level of economic activity is higher than expected, tax revenue will be higher and expenditure on benefits will be lower – so the result may be a negative PSBR.

Throughout the 1970s and up to 1986 the UK had a positive PSBR (see Figure 7). However, the Conservative governments were keen to lower the PSBR for the following reasons:

- *They wanted to reduce the growth of the money supply.* If the PSBR is financed by borrowing from the Bank of England or other institutions in the banking sector, the money supply will increase (see later in this chapter on financing the PSBR).
- *They wanted to reduce inflationary pressures.* These may occur if the PSBR results in a rise in aggregate demand which is not matched by a corresponding rise in aggregate supply.
- *They wanted to reduce crowding out.* This happens when public sector expenditure replaces private sector expenditure (see Chapter 5).

In the early 1980s the PSBR remained high as unemployment rose. It then fell owing to, among other factors:

- cuts in spending on houses;
- revenue from council house sales;
- revenue from privatization;
- rising incomes which increased the revenue from both direct and indirect taxation.

The early 1990s saw a return to a positive PSBR.

The public sector borrowing requirement

The PSBR is made up of the borrowing of three sectors:

- *the central government borrowing requirement* (**CGBR**);
- *the local government borrowing requirement* (**LGBR**);
- *the public corporation borrowing requirement* (**PCBR**).

In some years the size of the PSBR has been greatly affected by the conduct of fiscal policy. For instance, there was a sharp fall in the PSBR after the harsh budget of 1981. However, as indicated in Figure 6, in other years cyclical changes have outweighed fiscal policy changes. Keynesians believe that a PSBR resulting from a budget deficit can be an appropriate outcome of fiscal management of the economy. If households and firms save too much, they think the government should borrow the savings and re-inject them into the economy to increase the level of aggregate demand (**deficit financing**).

Monetarists, on the other hand, argue that a PSBR (especially a large one) can have harmful effects – including reducing confidence in the strength of a country's economy.

Fiscal and monetary policy

The traditional Keynesian view concentrated on the effects that a PSBR has on aggregate demand. It did not pay much attention to the monetary aspects of the PSBR, except for the indirect effect on the rate of interest. Monetarists place more attention on the monetary effects. However, all economists now recognize that there are close links between fiscal and monetary policy. *Fiscal decisions influence the size of the PSBR, and monetary policy decisions determine how the PSBR is actually financed.* For example, a decision to lower the growth of the money supply is likely to involve tight control on government borrowing, and hence influence the relationship between government spending and taxation.

Financing the PSBR

The PSBR can be financed in one of, or a combination of, four main ways. These are borrowing from:

- the non-bank private sector;
- the Bank of England;
- the banking sector;
- overseas.

The government borrows by selling government securities. These include Treasury bills, bonds and National Savings Certificates. Some government securities, such as National Savings Certificates, can be cashed in on demand, whilst others may just pay interest (e.g. Consols).

1. Borrowing from the non-bank private sector

The largest source of finance of a PSBR is borrowing from the non-bank private sector (e.g. pension funds). This is likely to have a neutral effect on bank lending and the money supply, because the increase in bank deposits arising from an increase in government spending will be matched by a fall in bank deposits of people and institutions withdrawing money to purchase the government securities.

However, some people argue that a disadvantage of this source is that it may be at the economic and political cost of higher interest rates. The interest rates on government securities have to be made attractive. This may force private sector firms, seeking finance, to raise their interest rates. In addition to the increased competition for funds driving up interest rates, the rise in national income – resulting from expansionary fiscal policy – may also put upward pressure on interest rates. As incomes rise the demand for money for transactions purposes will increase. If the money supply is not increased this may raise the rate of interest.

Some of the upward pressure on real interest rates and the risk of crowding out can be avoided by **accommodating monetary policy**. This would involve increasing the money supply. This may not be inflationary if there is spare capacity in the economy. The economy may be

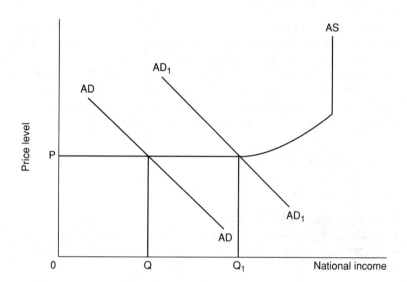

Figure 8 A non-inflationary increase in aggregate demand

operating on the horizontal part of the aggregate supply curve (see Figure 8), so that demand can rise and be matched by higher output.

Also, increased government borrowing may occur at a time when private investment is low (perhaps because of pessimistic business expectations), and using surplus investment funds will not, in this case, force up interest rates. Indeed there are many other factors which influence interest rates, and changes in the PSBR probably only have a small effect. Increasingly, local interest rates are influenced by world-wide capital market conditions and not just by domestic capital market conditions.

2. Borrowing from the Bank of England

Whilst selling government bonds to the non-bank private sector will not add to the money supply, increasing the note issue to finance the PSBR will. This is sometimes referred to as 'resorting to the printing press' and involves borrowing from the Bank of England. The Bank holds more bonds when it makes a loan to the government. The government increases the note issue and spends the money. The recipients of the government spending place the funds in their Bank accounts and the banks' operational balances at the bank of England rise. These balances are base (high-powered) money and enable the banks to increase their advances and hence the money supply.

3. Borrowing from the banking sector

The sale of Treasury bills to the commercial banks will also increase the money supply. When the government, through the Bank of England, sells Treasury bills to the banks, it receives funds which it then spends. The banks initially have less cash but have an equivalent value of Treasury bills. Both Treasury bills and cash are liquid assets and so the banks' liquid assets position is initially unchanged. However, as the recipients of the government spending deposit the funds with the commercial banks, the commercial banks' deposit holdings rise and they can lend more.

As both borrowing from the Bank of England and selling Treasury bills to the commercial banks lead to increases in banks' liquid assets and the money supply, they are together referred to as monetary finance.

4. Borrowing from abroad

One advantage of borrowing from aboard is that there is unlikely to be any crowding out. However, borrowing from abroad will involve, in the future, a transfer of income abroad, in the form of interest payable.

THE FULL-FUNDING RULE

In the 1980s the government, concerned about inflation, instructed the Treasury to fund the PSBR without making use of the banking sector. There were even some years in which the Treasury engaged in **overfunding**. This involved selling more government securities to the non-bank private sector than they needed in order to finance the PSBR. However, in the 1993 budget it was announced that some of the PSBR could be financed by borrowing from the banking sector. One motive behind this was the government's concern that the slow growth in the money supply was holding back economic recovery.

Reducing the PSBR

A government can seek to reduce a PSBR by:

- increasing revenue from national and local taxes;
- cutting public sector expenditure;
- increasing the profits or reducing the losses of nationalized industries;
- selling public sector assets such as nationalized industries (asset sales count as negative public spending and so directly cut borrowing).

A public sector debt repayment

A PSDR is a negative PSBR. It means that public sector income is greater than public sector expenditure and is likely to arise from a budget surplus. The surplus can be used to repay government debt by redeeming government securities, or to acquire other financial assets.

The initial effect of a PSDR is likely to be a reduction in bank lending as there will be a net withdrawal of funds from the banking system. Tax payers will be withdrawing more from commercial banks than

---

THE NATIONAL DEBT

The national debt is the accumulated past debt of the government. Considerable portions of the national debt are held by government funds and agencies. Other holders include commercial banks, the Bank of England and local authorities.

The national debt increases whenever the government spends more than it receives in taxes. A rise in the national debt will mean that the cost of **servicing** the debt (i.e. paying the interest and redeeming government securities) will increase. This may be financed by a rise in taxes and/or a rise in borrowing.

People often talk about the 'burden' of the national debt. Some even assume that a large national debt is a sign of economic weakness. This is not necessarily the case. What the standard of living of a country depends on is the quantity and quality of goods it is now producing.

Most of the national debt is held by UK citizens and as such involves an internal transfer from taxpayers to holders of the national debt. These may be the people who pay the most taxes. As we have seen, some argue that government borrowing may starve industry of funds and force up interest rates. However, empirical evidence does not suggest this occurs. In addition, Keynesian economists argue that increased public expenditure will generate higher income – and hence the tax revenue to cover the increased spending and interest payments.

Nevertheless, the size of the national debt may have some adverse effects. To the extent that taxes have to be raised to a level that is higher than would otherwise have been the case to pay for the debt, and these higher taxes act as a disincentive to work and innovate, it may prove to be a burden. In addition, transfers from taxpayers to debt-holders involves administrative costs (although these costs are likely to be small in comparison with the sums involved).

The part of the national debt which is held by foreigners may involve a transfer from domestic residents to overseas residents. Again, in this case, any burden is likely to be small because only about 10 per cent of the national debt is held abroad.

recipients of government spending will be depositing. However, the money supply and bank lending may not change if the effects are offset by the Bank of England buying government securities from the non-bank private sector.

A PSDR can raise the savings ratio when private sector saving is low.

An unbalanced budget will affect the size of the national debt. Whether this will have a beneficial or a harmful effect will depend on its cause, the state of the economy and how economic agents react.

KEY WORDS

Budget	PSDR
Reflationary fiscal policy	CGBR
Budget deficit	LGBR
Deflationary fiscal policy	PCBR
Budget surplus	Deficit financing
Fiscal stance	Accommodating monetary
Structural deficit	policy
Cyclical deficit	Monetary finance
Job seekers' allowance	Full-funding rule
FE budget concept	Overfunding
Public sector current financial	National debt
position	Servicing
PSBR	

Reading list

Healey, N., 'The PSBR', *British Economy Survey*, spring 1993.

Hurl, B., Chapter 6 in *Privatization and the Public Sector*, 2nd edn, Heinemann Educational, 1992.

Smith, D., Chapter 6 in *Mrs Thatcher's Economics: Her Legacy*, 2nd edn, Heinemann Educational, 1992.

Essay topics

1. (a) Distinguish between the PSBR and the PSDR.
   (b) In the financial year 1988–1989 the PSDR was £7bn. In the financial year 1992–93 the PSBR was £35bn. (i) Examine the circumstances which could account for these contrasting situations in the state of the government's finances. (ii) Analyse the economic consequences which might be expected to follow from such a marked change in the government's finances. (University of London Examinations and Assessment Council, 1994)

2. Explain the relationship between the PSBR and the national debt. Would there be any advantage to the UK in repaying the national debt? (Joint Matriculation Board, 1992)
3. Are budget deficits necessarily inflationary? (University of Oxford Delegacy of Local Examinations, 1990)

Data Response Question 3
The public sector borrowing requirement

This task is based on a question set by the Oxford & Cambridge Schools Examination Board in 1993. Study Tables A and B and answer the questions. (A suggested answer to this can be found in *Economics Today*, September 1993).

Table A Budget forecasts for the PSBR (£ billion)

Financial years	1990/91	1991/92	1992/93
1989 budget	-10	-6	-3
1990 budget	-7	-3	0
1991 budget	-1	8	12
1992 budget	-1	14	28

A negative figure indicates a public sector debt repayment.

Table B 1992 budget forecasts

Financial years	1991/92	1992/93	1993/94	1994/95	1995/96	1996/97
PSBR (£ bn)	14	28	32	25	19	6
PSBR as % of money GDP	$2\frac{1}{4}$	$4\frac{1}{2}$	$4\frac{3}{4}$	$3\frac{1}{2}$	$2\frac{1}{2}$	$\frac{3}{4}$
Annual growth of real GDP (%)	-2	2	$3\frac{1}{4}$	$3\frac{3}{4}$	$3\frac{1}{2}$	$3\frac{1}{4}$
GDP deflator (%)	7	$4\frac{1}{2}$	$3\frac{1}{2}$	3	$2\frac{1}{2}$	2

Source: Financial Statement and Budget Report.

1. Define PSBR. What factors influence its size?
2. Account for the revisions made by the government to its PSBR forecasts between the 1989 and 1992 budgets (Table A).
3. Why is the PSBR expected to continue to rise in 1993/94, despite a forecast increase in the rate of real GDP growth (Table B)?
4. What are the implications for macroeconomic policy of a rising PSBR (Table B)?
5. Why might some commentators regard the forecasts of a declining PSBR after 1993/94 as somewhat optimistic (Table B)?

Chapter Four

Stabilization policies

'Growth, employment and a better standard of living are the ultimate goals to which every aspect of economic policy must contribute.'
Kenneth Clarke, Chancellor of the Exchequer

Stabilization policies

Stabilization policies seek to ensure a stable growth in the level of aggregate demand to achieve certain macroeconomic objectives, including a high level of employment and price stability.

It is important to distinguish between **automatic stabilizers** which dampen a fall in aggregate demand during the downswing of the cycle and vice versa, and **discretionary stabilization policies**. The latter involve a more activist attempt to reduce fluctuations in the business cycle and may involve a deliberate increasing of a budget deficit during a time of low private sector aggregate demand.

As we will see, allowing the automatic stabilizers to work is only part of the standard Keynesian policy package. In the event of the economy becoming stuck in an unemployment equilibrium then more active policy measures are likely to be advocated.

Automatic stabilizers

Automatic stabilizers are those parts of government expenditure and tax revenues which move in a stabilizing direction in response to movements in national income. They prevent consumption falling as low or rising as high as it would otherwise have done and so act in a counter-cyclical manner. They reduce the multiplier effect of autonomous changes in private sector expenditure, boosting the economy during recessions and dampening it down during booms. For instance, as incomes rise, tax revenue (e.g. from income tax, corporation tax and VAT) will increase whilst government spending on, for example, housing and unemployment benefit will fall. This automatic tendency for the public sector to move into a smaller deficit or surplus during a boom will reduce sharp swings in economic activity.

Automatic stabilizers occur without any conscious changes in government policy being made. So there are no recognition or administrative lags involved (see the final chapter). However, automatic stabilizers can

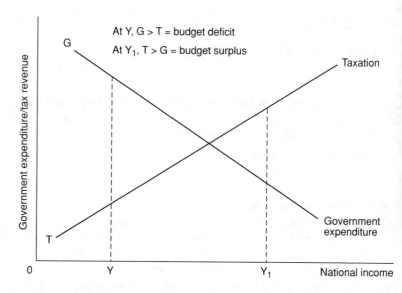

Figure 9 The effects on tax revenue and government expenditure of change in national income

still take time to work. For instance, as employment is thought to be a lagging indicator, rising some time after economic recovery occurs, it takes time for income tax revenue to increase.

Figure 9 shows the automatic tendency for tax revenue to rise and government expenditure to fall, as national income increases.

The role of automatic stabilizers

Until 1979 most economists and politicians believed automatic stabilizers should be allowed free rein to reduce cyclical fluctuations. So that income tax receipts would be allowed to fall during the downswing of the business cycle, government spending on, for example, unemployment and social security benefits would be allowed to rise and the budget deficit increase. However, some economists in the 1970s began to question the effectiveness of automatic stabilizers and their role in government policy. It was suggested, for instance, that state benefits may not actually act as an automatic stabilizer. A fall in unemployment may not reduce government spending on benefits if people have become more familiar with the benefit system whilst unemployed and have learned to claim more effectively. The attempt, between 1979 and 1981, by the government to reduce the budget deficit during a recession was a major departure from previous policy thinking. It involved reducing the power of automatic stabilizers to counteract cyclical fluctuations.

If a government maintains a fixed target for its public sector deficit position, it will reduce the effectiveness of automatic stabilization policy. Also, in effect the use of fiscal policy to manipulate aggregate demand is abandoned. *The operation of a fixed target may even make the operation of the public sector a destabilizing influence on the economy.* For instance, it may provoke a further downward spiral. If incomes fall thereby reducing tax revenue, and the government cuts its spending to maintain the same budget position, incomes may fall further. So government action may actually increase the multiplier effects of the autonomous changes in expenditure.

Keynesians argue that automatic stabilizers should be encouraged rather than resisted.

Demand management

Keynesians believe that if left to market forces, aggregate demand may be insufficient to achieve full employment or may be too high and lead to inflation. However, they think that **demand management** policies can be relied on to move the economy in the right direction.

Demand management involves using discretionary fiscal or monetary policy to ensure the appropriate level of aggregate demand. The government actually has a considerable influence on the broad components of total spending. Its own spending forms a relatively stable component of aggregate demand. It can also influence consumers' expenditure, which is the largest component of national income, the level of investment and exports by changing taxes and/or benefits.

A brief history of demand management

The principles of Keynesian demand management were introduced in wartime with the aim of lowering demand to free resources for the war effort and to avoid inflation. It was formally adopted in the 1944 budget and pursued by successive governments over the next three decades. In the 1950s and 60s, demand management policy tended to be short-term and very active as governments tried to achieve precise changes in the level of economic activity. It did have some success, with unemployment and inflation being relatively low in this period. However, there were balance of payments difficulties, often resulting in stop/go policies, and inflation became a serious problem in the 1970s. It was found difficult to use fiscal policies simultaneously against inflation and unemployment.

Some economists began to argue that the problems in implementing demand management tend to make it reinforce cyclical changes rather than act counter-cyclically. It was also argued that **monetary policy** and **supply-side measures** would be more effective in tackling the economy's difficulties. Indeed, by the mid 1970s traditional Keynesian demand management became increasingly unfashionable.

In a famous speech in 1976 to the Labour Party conference, the then Prime Minister, James Callaghan, cast serious doubt on the effectiveness of expansionary fiscal policy to reduce unemployment and warned of its potential inflationary effects:

> 'It used to be thought that a nation could just spend its way out of recession and increase employment by cutting taxes and boosting government spending. I tell you in all candour that that option no longer exists. In so far as it existed in the past, it had always led to a bigger dose of inflation, followed by a higher level of unemployment.'

Monetarist economists used the **expectations-augmented Phillips curve** to explain how government attempts to reduce unemployment by increasing aggregate demand only succeed in raising inflation. In Figure 10, SPC is the short-run Phillips curve, LPC is the long-run Phillips curve, and U_N is the natural rate of unemployment. In the short run, a rise in government expenditure lowers unemployment to U_1, but in the long run unemployment returns to U_N with an inflation rate of 5 per cent.

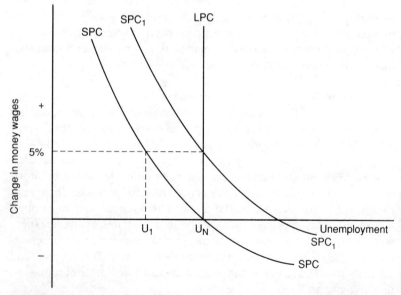

Figure 10 The expectations-augmented Phillips curve

Throughout the 1980s the government placed more reliance on monetary than fiscal policy. Controls were placed on government spending and changes in taxation were motivated more by a desire to reduce their distortionary and disincentive effects than to influence aggregate demand.

Fine tuning and coarse tuning
Fine tuning refers to short-term manipulation of aggregate demand that is intended to achieve very precise changes in economic variables, such as a fall of 1 per cent in unemployment and/or inflation.

Active fiscal policies of this kind pursued in the 1950s and 60s have come to be regarded as somewhat over-ambitious. To achieve small movements around the full-employment level would require very accurate information and very precise policy instruments.

There are now more modest views of what fiscal policy can achieve. **Coarse (or rough) tuning** involves infrequent changes in government policy implemented to achieve changes in demand aimed at moving the economy in the right direction whilst accepting that total accuracy cannot be guaranteed.

Effectiveness of demand management
Most economists agree that it would be very difficult for a government to manipulate aggregate demand so deftly as to ensure that full employment is always achieved. Where economists disagree is on how close demand management can permit a government to come to the ideal.

Keynesians believe that the private sector is inherently unstable. Large changes in private sector spending can occur, causing booms and slumps. They think that despite some problems in the past, governments now have the necessary information, forecasting techniques and instruments for demand management to be effective. So when there is a lack of private sector demand they argue that the public sector should borrow. Firms in the private sector borrow when it is considered appropriate and when it is believed the investment will generate the income which will pay the interest and create profit. They argue that the public sector should do the same. A rise in government spending, financed by borrowing, will raise national income by a multiple amount. As income

rises, government spending will fall while tax revenue will rise. So an increase in a budget deficit now is likely to reduce it in the future.

Monetarists and supply side economists are more sceptical about the effectiveness and appropriateness of discretionary demand management. They think it can add to, rather than reduce, cyclical fluctuations. They also believe that the cause of unemployment is not a lack of aggregate demand but labour market imperfections. They advocate, for instance, trade union reforms, and increasing the gap between unemployment benefit and wages, after tax, of the employed.

Rules

In the late 1970s and in the 1980s, monetarists came to favour the setting of medium-term rules for the conduct of government policy. Monetarists believe that discretionary policy changes are:

- unnecessary because the economy is essentially stable;
- difficult to operate because of, for example, time lags;
- undesirable because they increase the role of the state.

These economists see the role of the government as being confined to getting conditions right to allow the market economy to work unhindered. They believe the government is responsible for stable prices, via control of the money supply, and for legislation to allow markets to work freely. The rules they advocate for fiscal policy follow from their prescription for the money supply.

The monetarists' central rule for the money supply and how they believe inflation can be defeated is that the growth of the money supply should not exceed the growth of output. They consider that following rules will reduce inflation more quickly if people believe the government will keep to its measures to reduce inflation. They think that workers will moderate their wage claims and firms will be less likely to raise their prices. On the other hand, if a government does not follow a fixed rule, employers and employees may feel it will change its policy and so press for wage rises and raise prices in anticipation of inflation.

So monetarists think that fiscal and monetary policy should be designed to ensure that monetary growth matches the expected growth of output.

The long-term rules for fiscal policy which they advocate are a balanced budget and a reduction in the ratio of government spending to GDP. These are intended to ensure that the government neither 'crowds out' private sector investment and activity nor increases monetary growth. For a few years the UK's membership of **the ERM** provided a rule for monetary policy which also constrained fiscal policy (see Chapter 6).

THE ROLE OF BUDGETARY POLICY

CHRISTOPHER HUHNE

There is nothing wrong with using budgetary policy – taxes and spending – to support the economy during a recession. This covert piece of Keynesian pump-priming is one of the reasons why we are likely to enjoy a modest if halting recovery this year. The public sector's extra support for total spending in the economy this year alone is worth some 1.7 per cent of national income or £10.5bn, according to the OECD's calculations.

But the corollary of using budgetary policy actively in a recession is that the resulting deficit must be clawed back during the recovery: taxes have to rise, or public spending has to be restrained below the trend growth rate of the economy.

Source: Extract from 'Treasury meets its Waterloo', *Independent on Sunday*, 28 June 1992.

Discretionary fiscal policy versus rules

Whether economists favour **fiscal activism** or following rules depends on two key factors:

- how stable they believe the economy to be;
- whether they think there are serious problems involved in designing, implementing and operating stabilization policies.

Monetarists believe that the economy is inherently stable and that problems of fiscal policy are large. So they regard stabilization policy as being largely inappropriate. In contrast, as we have seen, Keynesians believe that the economy is inherently unstable and does not tend towards full employment. They think that it is better to attempt to offset such instabilities by counter-cyclical demand management policy despite the difficulties involved.

However, there are some areas of agreement. Even in a relatively stable economy there will be a role for fiscal policy. Intervention can be justified on the grounds of:

- the time required for the economy to return to high employment;
- the existence of shocks to the economy.

Indeed, fiscal policy has often been used to offset sudden unexpected changes in the economy (e.g. changes in the savings ratio; oil price movements; the 1987 stock market crash) in order to keep aggregate demand on a smooth upward path.

The medium-term financial strategy

The **medium-term financial strategy** (**MTFS**) was first introduced in 1980. In the MTFS the government sets out its targets for monetary growth and for public borrowing and seeks to ensure that its monetary and fiscal measures are consistent.

Balanced budget strategy

Monetarists believe that the main influence of a budget deficit will be on the money supply, and hence inflation, rather than on output and employment. As a result they argue that the budget should be balanced at a level of income consistent with an attainable level of employment. Some strict monetarists take the view that the budget should be in balance *each year*. At first this seemed to be the policy the Thatcher government was going to follow. However, the present declared aim of the government now is to balance the budget over the medium term, while allowing for a surplus in boom years and a deficit in recession years. The PSBR will thus vary with the cyclical position of the economy, permitting some discretionary management.

However, even a budget balance is no guarantee that there will not be deflationary or inflationary pressures resulting from fiscal policy. Different types of government expenditure and taxes will have different effects on the economy, and an equal rise in government spending and taxation will tend to increase aggregate demand (see the box 'Theory of the balanced budget multiplier'.

THEORY OF THE BALANCED BUDGET MULTIPLIER

Equal increases in government spending and taxation of, for example, £4 billion will increase the level of aggregate demand since, whilst injections will rise by £4 billion, withdrawals will rise by less than £4 billion. This is because some of the increase in taxation will be paid not by reducing expenditure on domestic goods but by reducing savings and spending on imports. So in part, one withdrawal would replace the other two withdrawals.

If the marginal propensity to consume of both taxpayers and the recipients of government expenditure is equal (e.g. 0.75), then national income will rise by the change in government expenditure and tax. There will be a net injection of £1 billion as government expenditure rises by £4 billion and private expenditure falls by £3 billion (taxpayers would have spent 0.75 x £4 billion of the rise in tax). National income changes by £1 billion (net injection) x 4 (the multiplier is 1/0 .25) = £4 billion.

The balanced budget also works in reverse, so that a fall in government expenditure and taxation of, for example, £6 billion will cause national income to fall by £6 billion.

Keynesians argue that what should be balanced at the full-employment level is total injections and withdrawals, and not just government spending and taxation. For instance, if at the full-employment level of income people wish to save more than firms wish to invest, government spending should be greater than taxation.

Weakness of rules

The main problem with rules is that it is difficult to find rules which will ensure good results in today's complex and changing economies. For instance it is difficult to control the money supply when it is difficult to define what money is in a society when the range of assets acting as money is increasing.

The idea that governments can improve the economy by foregoing independent policy action in favour of rules is at best unproven. A government is also unlikely to stick to rules over a long period of time.

After the ERM

For nearly two years the government's anti-inflationary strategy was based on sterling's membership of the Exchange Rate Mechanism (ERM) – see Chapter 6. Outside the ERM the strategy has changed to one of basing monetary policy on the prospective rate of underlying inflation. A target has been set for the underlying inflation of between 1 and 4 per cent.

The government is also pursuing a more active stabilization policy in seeking to achieve improvements in output, employment and living standards.

KEY WORDS

Automatic stabilizers	Keynesians
Discretionary stabilization policies	Monetarists
	Rules
Demand management	The ERM
Monetary policy	Fiscal activism
Supply-side measures	MTFS
Expectations-augmented Phillips curve	Balanced budget multiplier
Fine tuning	Balanced budget multiplier
Coarse tuning	

Reading list

Harrison, B., Smith, C., and Davies, B. Chapter 36 in *Introductory Economics*, Macmillan, 1992.

Healey, N., and Levačić, R., Chapter 5 in *Supply Side Economics*, 2nd edn, Heinemann Educational, 1992.

Sloman, J., Chapter 15 in *Economics*, Harvester Wheatsheaf, 1991.

Essay topics

1. (a) Outline the main macroeconomic objectives of the UK government in the 1990s. (b) Why do governments have difficulties in achieving these objectives? (University of London Examinations and Assessment Council, 1991)

2. Describe and comment on fiscal measures which may be taken by the government of your country to promote economic growth. (University of Cambridge Local Examinations Syndicate, 1990)

3. Can increased government expenditure reduce unemployment in: (a) the short run, and (b) the long run? (University of Oxford Delegacy of Local Examinations, 1992)

4. Assume an initial situation where there are unemployed resources and a balanced budget (i.e. government tax revenues are equal to its expenditure). (a) Explain why, other things being equal, an increase in government expenditure on goods and services of £1 billion might be expected to raise national income by an amount greater than £1 billion. (b) Given the present UK tax system, explain why an increase in government expenditure of £1 billion, with no change in tax rates, could increase the budget deficit by less than £1 billion, once the higher income level was achieved. (c) Suppose the government increased both its spending and its tax rates to keep its budget balanced. Why could this result in an increase in national income? (Welsh Joint Education Committee, 1992)

Date Response Question 4

The American experience

This task is based on a question set by the Associated Examining Board in 1991. Read the article below, which is extracted from a piece by Paul Craig Roberts in the *National Westminster Bank Quarterly Review* in February 1989, before answering the questions.

SUPPLY-SIDE ECONOMICS: AN ASSESSMENT OF THE AMERICAN EXPERIENCE IN THE 1980s

The supply-side policy in the United States was not designed to secure more revenues for the government or to balance the budget. It was directed towards overcoming the economy's inability to grow without rising inflation and toward reversing the decline in the competitive position of the United States. During the 1970s productivity growth declined sharply. Policymakers were confronted with worsening 'Phillips curve' trade-offs between inflation and unemployment, ending in both rising inflation and unemployment. In 1971 the US merchandise trade deficit turned negative and grew dramatically during the latter part of the decade despite the continuous fall in the dollar exchange rate.

Keynesian economists could not explain these developments or offer elected policy-makers an escape from the problems. This failure created an opportunity for supply-side economics, which argued that the policy of pumping up demand while neglecting incentives to produce had resulted in stagflation. As incentives were eroded, each additional increment of demand called forth less real output and more inflation. Supply-siders argued that improved incentives and less costs imposed by government would result in greater supply and more efficient use of productive inputs. The supply-side policy is an anti-inflationary one, because its goal is to increase real output relative to demand.

In the Keynesian approach, a fiscal change operates to alter demand in the economy. A tax rate reduction, for example, raises the disposable income of consumers. With government spending held constant, the increased consumer spending stimulates supply and moves the economy to higher levels of employment and gross national product. In this view, the size of the deficit determines the amount of the stimulus.

In contrast, supply-side economics emphasises that fiscal policy works by changing relative prices or incentives. High income tax rates and regulation are seen as disincentives to work and production regardless of the level of demand. As people respond to the higher after-tax income and wealth, or greater profitability, incomes rise and the tax base grows thus feeding back some of the lost revenues to the Treasury. The saving rate also rises, providing more funds for government and private borrowing.

1. What is meant by 'to balance the budget' in the first sentence?
2. What is meant by 'worsening "Phillips curve" trade-offs between inflation and unemployment' in the first paragraph?
3. Explain why the writer argues (at the end of the second paragraph) that 'supply-side policy is an anti-inflationary one, because its goal is to increase real output relative to demand'.
4. Examine the view put forward by some supply-side economists, that a cut in tax rates will not necessarily result in a fall in tax revenue.
5. Contrast Keynesian and supply-side economists' views of the way in which fiscal policy might be used to influence the level of national output and employment.

Chapter Five

Fiscal policy issues

'Ministers are hung up on the Treasury belief that curbing public borrowing will allow interest rates to fall. This may well be mythical – like the black cat in the dark room'   Samuel Brittan

Fiscal policy is a controversial area. Currently economists and politicians are debating a number of issues which relate to fiscal policy. These include whether public expenditure crowds out private expenditure, and what the present shortfalls of our fiscal system are and how it could be reformed.

The crowding out debate is concerned with the problems of whether fiscal expansion actually increases output and employment in the long run or whether it merely crowds out or replaces an equivalent amount of private expenditure, leaving total output unchanged. So **crowding out** occurs when *there is a transfer of resources from the private to the public sector.*

Arguments for the crowding out position

Among those economists who believe that crowding out will occur, there is disagreement as to its likely extent.

Complete crowding out will occur when private expenditure is reduced by the same amount that government expenditure is increased. In this case the **fiscal multiplier** is zero and the government cannot raise aggregate demand. So whilst the composition of national income changes, its size does not.

Some supply-side economists go further and suggest that a rise in government spending can actually *reduce* output and employment. They claim that this can occur when, as a result of employing more resources in less productive state activities, the government crowds out the wealth-creating activities of the private sector.

Others believe that there is likely to be *partial* crowding out so that income will rise by less than the rise in government expenditure. In this case there will be a fiscal multiplier of between zero and one. Higher government spending matched by an increase in taxation may reduce private sector consumption, and if it is financed by borrowing it may reduce private sector investment. This may occur for a variety of reasons:

- Open market sales of government securities may raise the rate of interest. This may discourage private sector consumption and marginal investment projects.
- The sale of extra government bonds may also lead to a fall in the quantity of finance available to private sector firms. This, however, presumes a high degree of substitution between government bonds and private sector shares and debentures.
- A budget deficit may also reduce private sector investment if it lowers business confidence.
- Higher government spending may reduce exports and hence employment in two possible ways. One is that a higher domestic interest rate may encourage a movement of **hot money** into the country. This may lead to an appreciation of a floating exchange rate which will raise export prices, in terms of foreign currency.
- The competitiveness of exports will also be reduced if inflation results from the increased public expenditure.

Those who believe that crowding out can occur, think that it can also work in reverse. A decrease in government spending may lower interest rates. This may stimulate new private sector investment and consumer expenditure and so offset, to a certain extent, the fall in aggregate demand arising from the contractionary fiscal policy.

Arguments against crowding out

Keynesians think that public spending does not reduce private sector expenditure. They argue that a rise in government expenditure will not reduce private sector investment if it generates extra funds for investment and if it does not raise interest rates (or if the investment is interest inelastic).

Indeed, public sector spending creates orders for the private sector. For instance, 90 per cent of civil engineering output is bought by the public sector. Keynes stressed that the level of savings is not fixed. He argued that investment creates savings and not vice versa. A rise in government expenditure, on for instance investment, will increase national income by a multiple amount (see Figure 11). As income rises extra savings are created to finance the higher level of government expenditure.

There is no empirical evidence that increased government borrowing involves a rise in interest rates, or vice versa as the quotation from Samuel Brittan argues. Over the years there have been widely diverging levels of real interest rates with given levels of borrowing. As we have seen in Chapter 3, there are a number of other, probably more important, influences on the rate of interest.

It is also questionable to what extent changes in interest rates affect

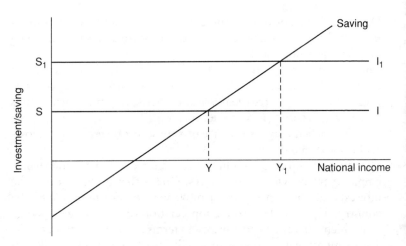

Figure 11 The effect of an increase in investment on savings

the level of investment. The most important influence on investment is thought to be changes in the level of aggregate demand. The **accelerator theory** states that what determines how much firms invest is the rate at which national income is rising or falling. It suggests that a change in national income will result in a greater percentage change in expenditure on capital goods. In estimating future demand for their products, entrepreneurs' expectations are very significant. Keynes referred to these as '**animal spirits**'.

Empirical evidence certainly suggests that complete crowding out does not exist. For instance, during the 1980s US administrations trebled the national debt as they increasingly overspent. Funding this debt by selling government bonds did not lead to a fall in private sector investment. Indeed, **crowding in** may occur with the increased activity and demand generated by deficits making entrepreneurs more optimistic and private sector investment more attractive.

Possible tax and expenditure reforms

A number of reforms have been advanced by economists to improve the fiscal system:

- Simplifying the system and reducing its administrative costs by incorporating National Insurance contributions into a unified system of income tax and removing the ceiling on contributions.
- 'Privatizing' the system as much as possible with the encouragement of private pension and health schemes.
- **Hypothecating** taxes. This would involve earmarking taxes for partic-

ular purposes (e.g. using fuel taxes for public transport). The link between taxation and spending would be clearer but there could be problems in matching revenue with perceived expenditure needs in particular areas.

- Introducing a **negative income tax**. This would be a simplified system incorporating the social security system and the tax system. Those above the threshold would pay positive income tax while those below it would receive payments. This, it is argued, would reduce the poverty trap (see below) as it avoids the sharp increase in marginal tax rates caused by flat rate benefits. It should also ensure automatic take-up of benefits. However, such a system may encourage employers to pay low wages knowing they would be made up by payments from the government.
- Changing income tax rates.
- Changing the balance between direct and indirect taxation.
- Targeting benefits.

The last three proposals are examined in detail below.

Changing income tax rates

The government's motive behind its cuts in income tax has been to increase aggregate supply by improving incentives. The government believes that lower direct taxes:

- reduce evasion and avoidance of taxes;
- reduce emigration of skilled workers;
- increase innovation and enterprise;
- promote harder work;
- encourage people to seek promotion;
- encourage people to study for higher qualifications.

In the 1988 budget, Nigel Lawson argued that high rates of income tax '*destroy enterprise, encourage avoidance and drive talent to more hospitable shores overseas*'. In this budget the top rate of income tax was cut from 60 to 40 per cent and the basic rate to 25 per cent. In the 1992 budget a new lower tax rate of 20 per cent was introduced, and the 1993 budget lowered the threshold for this.

The response to changes in income tax

Most studies have found that changes in income tax rates have very little effect on the number of hours worked. Indeed, the small difference found implies that the income effects outweigh the substitution effects, so that lower taxes will be associated with a small decrease in hours worked This complex matter is explained in some depth in a companion volume in this series, *Supply Side Economics*, second edition, by Healey and Levačić (pages 62–66).

In practice most people:

- may try to take into account a range of taxes;
- may not be certain of the exact rates they pay;
- will not be able to alter the number of hours they work.

However, certain groups may be affected more significantly, particularly if tax thresholds are raised rather than tax rates cut:

- Women currently working part-time up to the limit where they do not pay tax may work longer if the tax threshold is raised.
- The unemployed may be more willing to seek employment, but obviously, if there are no jobs available this may be ineffective.

A reduction in tax rates may also stimulate enterprise, since entrepreneurs are one group who are likely to be able to alter the hours they work.

The Laffer curve

This was first proposed by an American, Arthur Laffer, in the early 1970s to support his assertion that cuts in tax rates can lead to an increase in government receipts from taxation. He actually drew it on a napkin at an official dinner, to explain the idea to a congressman.

The **Laffer curve** in Figure 12 shows the expected relationship between total tax receipts and marginal tax rates. It suggests that at

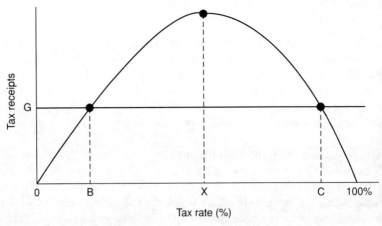

Figure 12 The Laffer curve

> ## TAX CUTS
>
> The Conservative party's philosophy is based on the idea that lower taxes encourage people to work harder and thus stimulate economic growth. According to this argument, higher growth will lead to more people being employed. This will allow the government to reduce what it spends on unemployment and social security benefits and will increase its tax revenues.
>
> The Labour party and others disagree with this analysis. They argue that there is little evidence to show that people work harder or longer when taxes are cut. In fact, they may choose to work less hard, because they will have to work a shorter number of hours for the same pay.
>
> Extract from 'At the hands of the tax collector', *The Guardian*, 25 Feb. 1992

very low and very high rates of tax, government receipts will be very low. At the extreme of a tax rate of 100 per cent, people cease to work and tax receipts will be zero. Apart from point X, there are always two points at which tax rates yield the same government revenue. For instance, government revenue of OG could be achieved at either tax rate OB or OC. Between X and C, high tax rates will stimulate tax evasion and discourage work. If the economy is at a point between X and C, a cut in tax rates will raise tax revenue.

The curve also suggests that there must be an average rate of tax which is the most efficient from the tax-gathering point of view.

There is little empirical evidence on the shape of the Laffer curve. For instance, it is possible that it is linear for much of its length, and it is also possible that there may be more than one peak. There is also considerable debate about where particular economies are on the curve. Indeed, if a country is at a point to the left of X, a cut in tax rates will reduce tax revenue. In practice it is difficult to construct just one curve from our complex tax system.

Tax avoidance and evasion

A number of economists advocate cutting tax rates in the belief that this will reduce tax avoidance and tax evasion.

Tax avoidance is legal but is inefficient. It involves the use of lawyers and accountants to find loopholes and tax privileges in the tax system to reduce the amount of tax paid.

Tax evasion involves concealment in one form or another of income earned and hence is fraud. VAT and excise duty are evaded but not on the same scale as income tax. However, the British are probably less guilty than many other nationals of tax evasion. *The extent to which GDP measured by the expenditure method exceeds GDP measured by the income method gives an indication of the extent of tax evasion.*

THE BLACK ECONOMY

The black economy consists of economic activity which is not recorded in national income figures, either because the activity itself is illegal (e.g. contract killing) or because the activities are not declared in order to avoid paying tax and/or losing benefit.

The size of the black economy is influenced by:

- the marginal rate of income tax;
- detection rates;
- punishments;
- public attitudes towards breaking or bending the tax laws;
- the size of the self-employed sector of the economy, where tax evasion is easier than in sectors where tax is deducted at source.

Some economists believe that a certain amount of tax evasion may be beneficial since it may enable certain goods and services to be produced that might otherwise not exist. However, if tax evasion becomes widespread, as it did with the Community Charge ('poll tax'), the tax will have to be reformed or replaced.

In addition to tax evasion leading to lower tax revenue, it has a number of other disadvantages:

- Economic activity goes unrecorded in official statistics and government policies may be based on inaccurate figures. The **Gutman effect** involves tax revenue rising when tax rates are reduced, owing to transactions previously in the black economy being entered in the official economy.
- There may be interference with the redistributive and allocative objectives of the tax system. For instance, a government's attempts to discourage consumption of a good by placing a high tax on it may not work if it is sold on the black market.

Direct versus indirect taxation

Most advanced countries, including the UK, are moving away from income tax towards greater reliance on indirect taxes. The UK government is pursuing this policy as it believes that indirect taxes have a lower **disincentive effect** on work effort, innovation and savings.

Indirect taxes have a number of other advantages over direct taxes. They can be varied more quickly and easily and take more immediate

SIN TAXES

'Sin' taxes are designed to discourage unhealthy living. The best known are the taxes on tobacco and alcohol products. These products have both VAT and high rates of excise duty imposed on them. The original purpose of imposing heavy taxes on these products was to raise revenue. They were seen as good sources of revenue as the demand for them is inelastic. However, one reason now for the continued relatively high level of tax on tobacco and beer, in particular, is that it acts as a form of social policy, reducing demand for demerit goods.

Smoking and drinking impose costs on consumers but also on third parties (negative externalities). The resulting diseases, including secondary cancer, cause pain and suffering to those afflicted and their families and impose a burden on the NHS and on the social security system (sick pay). The high consumption of alcohol causes road and other accidents and, by impairing the capability of workers and entrepreneurs, reduces the quantity and quality of output. Other costs to the community include the nuisance caused by the behaviour of drunken people in public places and air pollution caused by smoking.

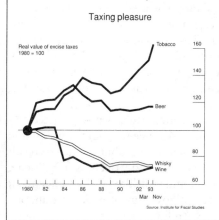

Taxing pleasure

Real value of excise taxes 1980 = 100

Tobacco

Beer

Whisky
Wine

1980 82 84 86 88 90 92 93
Mar Nov

Source: Institute for Fiscal Studies

effect. Since the Finance Act of 1961, the Chancellor of the Exchequer has had the power (via the **regulator**) to vary the rates of indirect taxation at any time between budgets. In contrast, direct taxes can only be changed at budget time.

However, indirect taxes have a number of disadvantages:

- They can be inflationary.
- They can distort consumer choice between taxed and untaxed goods.
- They are regressive, and the UK's greater reliance on indirect taxes has caused a redistribution of income to the rich.

Income redistribution

Income redistribution is influenced by transfer payments, subsidies and benefits in kind (e.g. education, health services). It is possible to put a monetary value on benefits in kind. These are sometimes referred to as the **social wage**. If high income earners benefit from the social wage to the same extent as low income earners, and at the same time contribute a higher proportion of their earnings in tax, then in effect there has been a redistribution of incomes even if no cash has been transferred from one group to another.

However, in practice expenditures on education and health tend to be consumed more by the rich than the poor and so create a greater inequality. The efficiency of the UK tax and benefit system in redistributing income in favour of the poor can be questioned on a number of other grounds. There is a confusion of benefits administered by a variety of bodies. Owing to lack of knowledge and a sense that benefits are demeaning, not all those entitled claim.

There is also the question of whether benefits should be based on a **universalist approach** or a **targeted** one. The first one would mean paying the benefits to everyone in a certain category, irrespective of income (e.g. National Insurance benefits). These are known as 'contingent payments'. This method is cheap to administer and avoids the problem of poor take-up. However, its total costs are high and payments are made to those who may not need them. So, in terms of reducing poverty, some of the expenditure is wasted.

The second approach uses income-related benefits paid only to individuals who are assessed as needing assistance (e.g. family credit and housing benefit). This method is cheaper in total, but it tends to result in a low take-up rate (thereby reducing its effectiveness in reducing poverty), it is expensive to administer and is disliked by its recipients. It is the method favoured by the present government which is unhappy with the growth of social security expenditure.

The poverty trap and the unemployment trap

The **poverty trap** affects the poorest members of society, especially those who do earn some income. It refers to people becoming worse off when their income rises and finding it difficult to escape from poverty through finding employment or through undertaking more work (see Figure 13). In effect they pay a marginal tax rate of over 100 per cent. Some poorer families on means-tested benefits find that, on receiving a pay increase, they pay extra tax and extra National Insurance, and they lose housing benefit and family income support. This can arise from a lack of coordination of tax and expenditure policies. (In the UK, taxes and benefits are administered by two different departments – the Treasury and the Department of Social Security.)

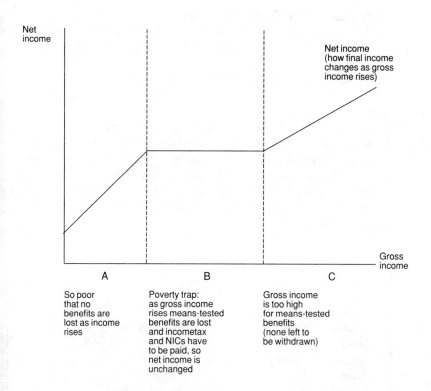

Figure 13 The poverty trap

The **unemployment trap** refers specifically to some people being better off being unemployed than being employed. It is thought that the unemployment trap applies to a only few; for instance some unskilled people with several children. Most people receive less on unemployment pay or social security benefit (which people move on to after being unemployed for more than a given period) and there are social pressures to find employment.

The poverty trap can influence wage determination. Low-paid workers may have to press for large wage rises in order to overcome the poverty trap, and employers may seek to keep wage rises down on the grounds that the net gain from an increase in wages is much smaller than the gross amount. The 1988 budget reduced the possibility of families facing marginal tax rates of 100 per cent. This was achieved by relating benefits to net income after tax and taking the previous benefits paid into account. However, marginal tax rates of over 90 per cent still exist.

Changes in the fiscal system

The future operation of fiscal policy will be influenced by ministers' views on the crowding out issue and the relative merits of possible reform to the fiscal system.

As the quote from Samuel Brittan suggests, many economists now question whether interest rates are affected to any great extent by government borrowing.

Pressure to improve our fiscal system is coming from concern about the continued upward movement in public expenditure (see Chapter 2) and a general consensus that our system contains a number of shortcomings. Where economists disagree is about how improvements should be achieved. The next few years are likely to witness vigorous debate about, for example, the merits of hypothecating taxes and targeting benefits.

KEY WORDS

Crowding out	Gutman effect
Fiscal multiplier	Black economy
Hot money	Disincentive effect
Accelerator theory	Regulator
Animal spirits	Sin taxes
Crowding in	Social wage
Hypothecating	Universalist approach
Negative income tax	Targeted approach
Laffer curve	Poverty trap
Tax avoidance	Unemployment trap
Tax evasion	

Reading list

Beardshaw, J., Chapter 41 in *Economics: A Student's Guide*, Pitman, 1992.

Hamilton-Jones, T., 'Indirect taxes', *Economics Today*, January 1994.

Healey, N., and Parker, D., Chapter 5 in *Current Topics in Economics*, Anforme Ltd., 1990.

Healey, N., and Levačić, R., Chapter 5 in *Supply Side Economics*, 2nd edn, Heinemann Educational, 1992.

Keefe, J., 'Direct versus indirect taxes', *Economics Today*, September 1993.

N.I.E.S.R., Chapter 4 in *The UK Economy*, 2nd edn, Heinemann Educational, 1993.

Whynes, D., Chapter 3 in *Welfare State Economics*, Heinemann Educational, 1992.

Wilkinson, M., Chapters 7 and 8 in *Equity and Efficiency*, Heinemann Educational, 1993.

Essay topics

1. In 1978 the standard rate of income tax was 33 per cent and the top rate was 83 per cent; in 1990 the standard rate was 25 per cent and the top rate was 40 per cent. Examine the likely economic consequences of these changes. (University of London Examinations and Assessment Council, 1992)

2. 'The United Kingdom taxation and welfare benefit systems have trapped the low-waged in relative poverty and the unwaged in unemployment.' Explain the causes of this situation, and how problems created might be reduced. (Associated Examining Board, 1991)

3. (a) What is meant by the 'equilibrium level of national income'?
   (b) What are the main determinants of the level of national income in a closed economy with no government sector?
   (c) How can the government use fiscal policy to influence the equilibrium level of the national income?
   (d) It is sometimes claimed that too high levels of government spending will 'crowd-out' (i.e. reduce) private sector investment. Explain why this may be so. (Northern Ireland Schools Examinations and Assessment Council, 1992)

4. (a) Under what circumstances might a government decide to increase taxes?
   (b) What criteria are relevant when considering the relative merits of direct and indirect taxes? (University of London Examinations and Assessment Council, 1991)

5. Outline the functions of taxation. Discuss the likely effects upon the behaviour of households of a switch from direct to indirect taxation. (Joint Matriculation Board, A/S level, 1991)

6. 'A policy of reducing income tax rates in order to increase labour market incentives may sometimes increase the supply of labour, but it can also lead to less labour being supplied.' Discuss. (Associated Examining Board, 1990)

Data Response Question 5

Poverty in Britain

This task is based on a question set by the Oxford & Cambridge Schools Examination Board in 1990. Read the two extracts below and answer the questions.

Poverty in Britain has increased sharply since 1979, and a growing proportion are long-term poor. By 1985 (the latest available figures), 9.4 million people, including 2.25 million children, were living at or below the official poverty line. This is 17% of the population – an increase of 55% since 1979.

In 1985, over 15 million people were living in poverty or on its margins (up to 40% above the Supplementary Benefit [now Income Support] scale. This is 28% of the population.

In 1989, half a million families are caught in the poverty trap. For a couple with two children, if gross weekly earnings rise from £30.40 (when Housing Benefit starts to fall) to £165.90 (when Family Credit runs out), net income only rises from £126.20 to £143.70. An earnings rise of £135.50 increases net income by only £17.50. The effect of means-tested benefits is equivalent to a marginal tax rate of 87% over the whole income range.

Source: *Fabian Society*, 1989

Are the poor 'getting poorer'? No, they are not. It is clear that people at all income levels now have substantially more money to spend in real terms than they did in the 1970s. In fact by almost every material measure it is possible to contrive – health, longevity, real income, ownership of consumer durables, number and length of holidays, money spent on entertainment, numbers in further education – not only are those with lower incomes not getting poorer, they are substantially better off than they have ever been before. Strong economic growth, coupled with cuts in income tax, have helped raise living standards to record levels. For a family with two children in the bottom 10% of the earnings league real take-home pay has risen by almost 14% since 1979. The real incomes of the poorest tenth of the whole population rose by 8.3% between 1981 and 1985 (the latest available figures). Total spending on benefits has now increased in real terms since 1978/9.

Source: *Conservative Research Department*, 1989

1. Define the following, all of which appear in the Fabian Society extract:
   (a) official poverty line
   (b) Income support
   (c) poverty trap
   (d) net income
   (e) marginal tax rate.
2. What light do the above extracts throw on the causes of poverty in Britain? Can these arguments over the extent of poverty be reconciled?

Chapter Six

Fiscal policy and the European Union

'There is now an energetic debate about the European Community in Britain and indeed throughout Europe. I welcome this.'   John Major

The EU and the UK's budget position

Membership of the European Union (EU) affects domestic UK taxation in two main ways:

- a certain amount of tax revenue has to be paid to the EU;
- the structure and rates of certain taxes are influenced by the requirements of the EU.

The UK's membership also affects UK public expenditure and the UK budget position. For instance, Article 104c of the Treaty on European Monetary Union (**Maastricht Treaty**) requires that member states

'shall avoid excessive governmental deficits'.

If a member state refuses to comply, the council can

'invite the European Investment Bank to reconsider its lending policy towards the member state concerned' or 'impose fines of an appropriate size'.

The EU is afraid that if a few countries run large budget deficits, they may cause problems for other member countries. If they finance their deficits by borrowing they may absorb too much of the savings undertaken in the EU, and if they finance it by borrowing from the banking sector they may cause inflation which may be imported into other EU countries. The Maastricht target is that deficits should be reduced to 3 per cent of GDP.

In addition to regarding it as sound economic management to keep deficits low, the EU sees this limit as a movement towards the final stage of **European Monetary Union** (EMU).

However, it is doubtful whether the EU will enforce the 3 per cent figure as it is regarded by many economists and politicians as being too low and too rigid. Indeed, the EU is likely to raise it in the near future and to allow variation between countries to allow for differences in countries' structural and cyclical positions. For instance, countries have different savings ratios and may be experiencing different levels of private sector aggregate demand.

The EU budget

The **EU budget** is small relative to most countries' GDPs. However, it can have a noticeable effect on members' economies and is a rather controversial area. There are regular disputes between member countries and the EU, and between EU institutions, about the size and composition of the budget. The EU budget has four sources of revenue:

- the customs duties of the common external tariff;
- agricultural import levies;
- an amount equivalent to 1.4 per cent of VAT;
- up to 1.2 per cent of each member country's GNP, as an annual transfer.

The contributions are assessed each year. Approximately 58 per cent of the revenue comes from VAT, 22 per cent from customs duties, 9 per cent from GNP-based resources and only 6 per cent from levies on agriculture.

Spending by the EU relative to the total levels of government spending in member countries is also small, accounting for only about 1–2 per cent of the GDP of member states. This contrasts with national government budgets which are usually between 32 and 43 per cent of GDP. However, this spending can have a significant impact on some sectors of the member countries' economies.

The UK's net contribution to the EU budget

In 1991 the net contributors to the EU budget were the UK, Belgium and Germany. The other nine members were net beneficiaries. In 1991 the UK paid £5807 million:

- £1731m in agricultural levies and duties
- £3801m based on VAT receipts, and
- £813m based on the level of GDP minus £538m refund for overpayment in 1990.

The UK received £5261 million:

- £1761m payments relating to agriculture
- £615m from the social fund
- £388m from the regional development fund, and
- £2497m in an annual rebate.

So it made a net contribution of £546 million. The differences between member state contributions reflect two main factors. First there are different patterns of VAT revenues, which in turn reflect the levels of consumer spending in each member state. The richer countries tend to have higher consumer spending and so higher VAT payments. The second factor is the customs duties paid on imports from outside the EU, known as the common external tariff (CET).

The UK is a net contributor because of the way the EU budget is structured. As agriculture accounts for the largest share of the EU's expenditure, and more revenue comes from countries which have higher consumer spending and import a large amount from outside the EU, the system works best for countries which have large agricultural sectors, are net exporters of agricultural products and trade very little with countries outside the EU. The UK imports food, has a small farming sector and, although most of our important trading partners are in the EU, we still trade to a considerable extent with non-EU countries, for instance the USA.

The UK does not do well out of the Common Agricultural Policy (CAP). France is the main beneficiary of that. However, the UK does better in other areas of EU spending, partly because of its economic problems. Almost a quarter of EU spending goes on **structural funds,** which are planned to increase in the future. These are used for regional and social development. There is aid for regions suffering from industrial decline, lagging behind other regions, and for the promotion of development in the rural areas. The UK benefits particularly in terms of regions suffering from industrial decline, receiving 38 per cent of the total spent in the period 1989–93.

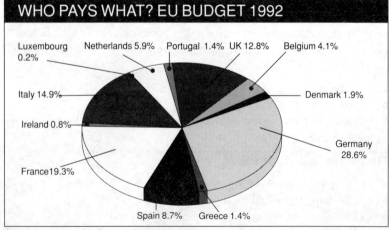

WHO PAYS WHAT? EU BUDGET 1992

Luxembourg 0.2%
Netherlands 5.9%
Portugal 1.4%
UK 12.8%
Belgium 4.1%
Italy 14.9%
Denmark 1.9%
Ireland 0.8%
Germany 28.6%
France 19.3%
Spain 8.7%
Greece 1.4%

Source: Commission of the European Communities

Nevertheless the UK government has been unhappy about the net amount it has had to pay. So since 1984 the UK has had a rebate amounting to two-thirds of the net difference between what it pays in and what it gets in return. The rebate was won by Margaret Thatcher at the 1984 Fontainebleau summit. Some of the EU members would like the rebate to disappear but obviously the UK wants it to stay.

Fiscal harmonization

Under the terms of the Single European Act 1985 there is a target of fiscal harmonization in the EU. **Fiscal harmonization** means reducing differences in taxes between member states and can involve both direct and indirect taxes. It has a number of stages. The first is agreeing the *tax type*. The EU has, for instance, agreed on VAT rates. Then there is harmonization of the *tax base* and harmonization of *tax rates*. These two steps can proceed side by side.

It is anticipated that fiscal harmonization in the EU will:

- enhance competition on equal terms;
- promote free trade and hence permit greater advantage to be taken of comparative advantage;
- move the community towards greater economic and political integration.

Differences in corporation taxes and taxes on labour can affect the investment and location patterns of firms. Without tax harmonization countries may engage in a comparative reduction of taxes, in order to attract companies. Companies, in particular **multinationals**, may seek the maximum grants and minimum taxes. This situation is unlikely to result in the best tax structures.

For harmonization of income tax to be meaningful, there would have to be harmonization of social security and pension contributions and possible social security benefits. However, there is a tacit agreement that at the moment personal income tax should remain under the jurisdiction of the individual countries, and the current UK government is opposed to the harmonization of European welfare standards and is the one member country of the Community to refuse to sign the **Social Chapter**. The key features of the Social Chapter include seeking to achieve the convergence of welfare payment systems of the member states, setting minimum criteria for holiday entitlements, overtime and length of the working week, and the introduction of a minimum wage.

Harmonization of indirect taxes

At present the EU is concentrating on indirect taxes. There is currently considerable variation, particularly in terms of excise duties on alcohol and tobacco. There are also differences in the VAT rates in different countries, in terms of the number of rates in operation and their levels. However, in all countries, exports are zero-rated and imports are taxed in the same way as domestic products. *So, in theory, there is no explicit discrimination by any one member state against the products of another in the operation of the VAT system.*

Nevertheless the existence of different rates of VAT and other sales taxes can act in a discriminatory way. For instance, low taxes on beer but high taxes on wine will stimulate the UK beer sales to the disadvantage of imports of wine from France and Germany. It is important to keep cross-border shopping down to a reasonable level so that countries do not lose significant amounts of tax revenue. To achieve this the differences in national tax rates will have to be reduced.

However, moving towards a common EU pattern of indirect taxes will remove some of the sovereignty of countries' fiscal policy. Countries may actually want to set different tax rates because they have different needs and objectives.

Recent developments

In July 1992 it was agreed that the legally binding minimum rate of VAT in EU countries should be 15 per cent until the end of 1996. No maximum rate was set. The EU directive permits member countries to introduce one or more reduced rates in a band between 5 and 15 per cent on a list of items. In addition the UK has special permission to bring any of the items it currently zero-rates into the reduced-rate band. As with the other member countries, the UK can also choose to keep existing zero rates in force. The minimum rate will be reviewed in 1995, and if an agreement cannot be reached, no legally binding minimum will be set.

The then Chancellor, Norman Lamont, conceded that the UK's minimum rate of VAT would henceforth be determined in Brussels. However, he also stated that as the minimum rate is below the UK's VAT rate of 17.5 per cent, '*there is no chance of the new rules constraining the government.*' Minimum duties on a range of other products including tobacco, alcohol and heating oils were also agreed. Without an accord EU members might have been tempted to make unilateral changes in VAT rates, aimed at attracting cross-border shoppers.

Future movements towards fiscal harmonization

In practice there is likely to be a balance between achieving greater economic neutrality between member states whilst retaining a relatively high degree of **national sovereignty** in tax policy. So tax harmonization

---

The 'Granny Tax'

In the March 1993 budget the Chancellor announced that VAT would be charged on domestic fuel and power at 8 per cent from 1 April 1994 and at the full standard rate (17.5 per cent) from 1 April 195. The Chancellor gave three reasons for extending the VAT on to heating:

- to encourage the efficient use of fuel;
- to reduce the emission of carbon dioxide;
- to raise revenue.

This move was heavily criticized because the tax falls more heavily on the poor, and particularly on the elderly as they spend a higher proportion of their income on heating. On the day after the budget the government stated that extra help would be given to people on low incomes but waited until the November 1993 budget to announce increases in:

- benefits for the disabled, the poor and all pensioners
- cold weather payments
- the grant scheme for insulating low income homes and widening it to cover all pensioners and people receiving disability benefits.

---

may be aimed at unifying some taxes whilst having a co-ordinated but differential approach to others.

Some tax differences can remain without resulting in a high-tax-rate country losing revenue to a country with a lower rate. This is particularly the case for the UK because of the transport costs necessarily involved in cross-border trade. It seems likely that the UK could maintain zero-rating on food independently of the rest of the EU without tempting shoppers from the continent.

The Exchange Rate Mechanism (ERM)

The UK has been a member of the **European Monetary System (EMS)** since it was set up in December 1978, but did not join the most important feature of it, the ERM, until October 1990.

In the 1992 budget the Chancellor stated that the central plank of the government's economic policy was membership of the ERM. The role of fiscal policy in the ERM was to ensure that aggregate demand did not grow faster than aggregate supply, through operating a balanced budget in the medium term.

However, UK membership of the ERM was suspended in September

1992 and the mechanism has since come under further pressure. The government has stated that the UK will not rejoin the ERM until the economic performances (including interest rates) of the members, particularly the UK and Germany, are closer.

Full membership of the ERM removes some of the government's power to take unilateral action in fiscal policy. Major changes have to be discussed at community level and countries often have to modify

their views to obtain a consensus. Countries can still have various levels of budget deficit and different tax or public expenditure to GDP ratios, but the size and direction of annual changes in fiscal policy will be influenced by monetary policy decisions determined by the ERM.

In the mid-to-late 1980s, before UK membership of the ERM, the government in effect used the rate of interest as a fine-tuner. In this period the ratio of borrowing to income had risen which made firms and households more sensitive to interest rate changes. However, when the UK entered the ERM, it lost some of its power to alter the rate of interest for domestic purposes.

Indeed, there can be periods when the interest policy needed to keep a currency within the ERM margins clashes with that required for management of the domestic economy. The objective of interest rate management tends to change from influencing internal monetary growth to maintaining the exchange rate. One of the advantages claimed for leaving the ERM in the autumn of 1992 was that the government could cut the rate of interest significantly in an attempt to stimulate the economy. The government is also now freer to pursue a more expansionary fiscal policy as less attention has to be paid to how the currency markets view changes in fiscal policy. However, some economists argue that this has removed some disciplinary pressure on the government to follow prudent fiscal policies. Although membership of the ERM limits the independence of national interest rate policy, it may make fiscal policy more flexible and more important. For instance, if interest rates have to be high to protect the value of the currency at a time of low aggregate demand, fiscal policy can be relaxed.

Future developments

In the event of full monetary and economic union there would no longer be independent national monetary policy. It would be established for the Community as a whole by a **European Central Bank**. There would be one currency and a single set of interest rates, uniform across the member countries. So what would be left of macroeconomic policy at the national level would be fiscal policy. Indeed, the **subsidiarity principle** (i.e. getting the right balance between Community and national action, with the EU involving itself only in matters with which it can deal more effectively than the governments of the individual countries) which is enshrined in the Maastricht treaty, suggests that as much of fiscal policy as possible should be left in the hands of national governments.

In the very long run there may be a reduction of national fiscal sovereignty. The EU may seek to co-ordinate fiscal policies to avoid, for example, one country's expansionary fiscal policy affecting other members' economies in a way they do not want. However, the transfer of monetary sovereignty will be completed first and is in its early stages now, albeit with some setbacks, with members of the ERM having their freedom to change their interest rates limited.

The EU's own budget is also likely to remain relatively small in terms of GDP for some time. During this period fiscal policy will become more important as a national government will have more ability to use this form of macroeconomic policy, rather than most other forms, to achieve its domestic objectives.

The debate about the effect of the EU on UK domestic policy and of UK domestic policy on the EU will continue to be vigorous.

KEY WORDS

Maastricht treaty	Social Chapter
European monetary union	National sovereignty
EU budget	ERM
Structural funds	EMS
Fiscal harmonization	European Central Bank
Multinationals	Subsidiarity principle

Reading list

Hill, B., *The European Community*, 2nd edn, Heinemann Educational, 1994.

N.I.E.S.R., *The UK Economy*, 2nd edn, Heinemann Educational, 1993.

Sloman, J., Chapter 21 in *Economics,* Harvester Wheatsheaf, 1991.

Essay topics

1. Compare the alternative ways open to the government to influence the level of economic activity. Explain what effect, if any, membership of the ERM has upon the government's choice of policy instruments. (Joint Matriculation Board, 1991)

2. In October 1990 the UK joined the Exchange Rate Mechanism of the European Monetary System. In what ways might entry into the ERM affect the UK economy? (Welsh Joint Education Committee, 1992)

3. 'British membership of the European Exchange Rate Mechanism is a strategy designed to reduce the rate of inflation at the expense of domestic output and employment.' Discuss. (Oxford & Cambridge Schools Examination Board, 1991)

4. (a) Contrast the impact of monetary and fiscal policies which a government might use to rectify a worsening balance of payments on current account. (b) How has the UK's membership of the ERM affected the government's freedom of action in the use of these policies? (University of London Examinations and Assessment Council, 1993)

5. (a) How is Britain's contribution to the European Community budget determined? (b) Is it reasonable to expect Britain to pay a larger contribution in the future? (Oxford & Cambridge Schools Examination Board, 1993)

6. What do you understand by the phrase 'conflict of policy objectives'? To what extent is the UK's ability to pursue domestic economic poli-

cies limited by balance of payments constraints? (University of London Examinations and Assessment Council, 1991)

Data Response Question 6

The Maastricht Treaty and EMU

This task is based on a question set by the Oxford & Cambridge Schools Examination Board in 1993. Read the article below, which is adapted from a piece by Andrew Britton entitled 'From EMS to EMU' (IEA: *The State of the Economy 1992*), before answering the questions.

Attempts to conduct an independent macroeconomic policy in Britain are now seen as a failure. A European monetary union, with a single currency, is now seen as the most reliable route to price stability.

The institutional framework for monetary union, as agreed at Maastricht, has been built mainly to a German model. *The proposed European central bank will be largely independent of government,* and therefore able to distance itself somewhat from political pressure. The over-riding aim of monetary policy, written into the constitution of the bank, will be price stability – i.e. a rate of inflation of about 2 or 3% a year. The Maastricht Treaty defines, precisely and arithmetically, just what *measures of convergence* are needed before individual countries are deemed fit to join a monetary union.

Clearly, any unified central mechanism must involve setting uniform interest rates. Indeed, the main instrument by which price stability will be secure will be the setting of these interest rates. Even in a monetary union, *the rate of inflation will not be identical in each country* and anxiety remains that the cost of achieving permanently low inflation will turn out to be very high for the countries with a history of relatively high inflation.

The case for monetary union rests on the belief that adjustments of imbalances between member countries is possible without changing exchange rates. Countries which become uncompetitive should reduce real wages or raise productivity so as to maintain or restore *full employment.* Within a nation state the problem of maintaining regional balance is solved in part by *fiscal transfers,* which help to narrow the regional dispersion of real incomes and employment levels. No such transfers are envisaged within EMU. The Treaty makes provision for some enlargement of the *regional and social funds,* but these are not designed to bail out the industries of countries which fail to reduce inflation and thus price themselves out of the European market. These funds will therefore do nothing at all to ease Britain's path to full membership of EMU. Now that exchange rates cannot move to compensate for lack of competitiveness, the main burden of adjustment must rest with wage and price flexibility.

1. Give three examples of 'attempts to conduct an independent macro-economic policy in Britain'.

2. Define (i) full employment; (ii) fiscal transfers; (iii) regional and social funds.
3. What are the advantages of having a European central bank that is 'largely independent of government'?
4. What is meant by 'measures of convergence' (second paragraph)? Why is such convergence seen as a precondition of EMU entry?
5. 'Clearly, any unified central mechanism must involve setting uniform interest rates'. Why?
6. Why will the rate of inflation 'not be identical in each country'?
7. Why does the author believe that Britain's path to full membership of EMU might be difficult? What options are open to a government to smooth this path?

Chapter Seven

Local government

'Local taxation has long been a controversial and somewhat unsatisfactory area of British finance.'   M. Artis

Levels of fiscal policy

Changes in public sector expenditure and taxation can occur at a number of different levels. The European Union spends and receives revenue from taxes raised in the Union (see Chapter 6). Within the UK, at a national level, government departments and public corporations spend, and the Inland Revenue and the Customs and Excise departments levy taxes. At another level local authorities spend and raise revenue.

Balance of spending

There are arguments for and against changing the balance of expenditure between central government and local authorities. Increasing the proportion spent by central government represents a move towards **centralization**. The advantages of this include:

- making it easier to achieve central government objectives;
- taking advantage of economies of scale;
- reducing the problem of co-ordination between areas, making it easier, for example, to deal with externalities arising from one area polluting another.

However, there are also arguments for **decentralization**:

- local authorities are closer to people and so may be more aware of their preferences;
- local authorities may be in a better position to react quickly to changes in tastes and wants;
- local variations in the provision of services may increase innovation and efficiency, with good practice spreading.

It would be easier to decide the optimum balance of central and local government activity if it was possible to divide services clearly into those which benefit people within an area and those which benefit everyone in the country. However, this is very difficult since people and vehicles move. For instance, local spending on a new road may benefit a large number of people who live outside the area.

Local government spending

Local authorities spend on a variety of activities. For most the highest proportion, often a half, of their spending goes on education. However, this is changing. FE, tertiary and sixth form colleges have been financed, since April 1993, by the Treasury, via the Further Education Funding Council, and secondary schools are encouraged to opt out of local authority control. Other main areas of spending include social services, the police, highways, the fire service, libraries and waste collection and disposal.

Ability to pay versus benefit principle

Local authorities have to take a number of factors into account when deciding how to raise finance. These include:

- costs of collection;
- administration;
- buoyancy of revenue;
- fairness;
- accountability;
- effects on allocative efficiency.

They also have to decide on whether to base their taxes on the principle of ability to pay, the benefit principle or a combination of both.

The **ability to pay principle** assumes that fairness relates to the ability to pay and so people with higher incomes should pay more.

The **benefit principle** argues that people should pay taxes related to the benefit they derive from public expenditure. So the benefit principle is related to peoples' willingness to pay. Consumers would pay an amount based on the quantity they consume as they do for goods purchased through the market. This principle works best in the case of services which could be provided privately and which have no significant externalities. However it works less well when it is difficult to calculate who benefits and how much people benefit from particular services, for example public parks. The benefit principle might be thought to be closely connected to the ability to pay principle. This is because as peoples' ability to pay increases their willingness to pay for normal goods will be likely to increase. However, the relationship may not be that close, and may sometimes move in opposite directions. It may be the case that the rich place low values on publicly provided services, and hence have a low willingness to pay.

Ways of raising finance

The main source of local authority's finance is central government grants. Other sources are taxes on firms, council tax and direct charges for services, (e.g. for the hire of a council hall). In the 1980s local authorities also obtained revenue as a result of the central government encouraging council house sales and the privatization of, for instance, leisure centres.

There has been, for some time, a debate about the best tax base for local authorities. The possibilities include taxing people per head, taxing incomes, taxing spending and/or taxing property.

A local sales tax

A **local sales tax** (i.e. a tax on the retail sales of goods and services in the local authority area) would be likely to be a percentage of tax in addition to VAT. Whilst it might not be expensive to collect it would have a number of disadvantages. These include its regressive nature, the inflationary impact it may have (at least in the short run), and it may distort production and consumption between local authorities. If a sales tax did vary between areas, there would be cross-border shopping with people living in high-tax areas shopping in neighbouring low-tax areas. This would result in resources, including petrol and travel time, being used just to avoid high tax levels. A vicious circle might develop: local authorities with regional shopping centres within their boundaries would benefit at the expense of their neighbours. So areas without large shopping complexes might have to levy a higher sales tax. This in turn would cause more people to shop outside the area. So a local authority could not set its rates significantly higher than neighbouring authorities and its autonomy to set the tax rates they want would be reduced. Also, whilst essentials such as food, which form a higher proportion of poorer households' spending, might not be taxed, those on benefits who do not pay income tax would nevertheless pay the sales tax and so could be the main losers from a sales tax.

A local income tax

A local income tax would have a number of advantages:

- It would be a progressive tax.
- There would be no need for a rebate system, as low-income families would automatically pay low amounts, or even in some cases, nothing.
- The amount collected would increase every year as incomes rise, thereby avoiding the need for frequent increases in the tax rate.

There would, however, be the question of how the tax would be administered. It could be collected either by the Inland Revenue at the same time as income tax is collected, or by the local authorities themselves, perhaps making use of income details supplied by the Inland Revenue. It would increase the burden of direct tax, raising the marginal rate of income tax. Some economists believe this would reduce the incentive to work. Differences in spending between local authorities would lead to variations in tax rates. This might encourage people to move to the low-taxed areas. In addition, the burden of a local income tax would be placed on approximately 20 million out of 35 million voters in England, which some believe is not adequate to achieve local authority accountability.

Property tax

The main advantages of a property tax are:

- There are low administration costs owing to the ease of collection and relatively low number of taxpayers.
- There is no overlap with neighbouring areas.
- As property is immobile, this makes enforcement easier.
- It involves some element of ability to pay because richer people will tend to buy more expensive houses.
- It does not act as a disincentive to work because it does not alter the marginal rate of tax.
- It gives an incentive to make fuller use of housing since, in effect, it falls with each extra occupant.
- There are already at national level taxes on income and capital gains but not on the returns received from owning property. These include a flow of housing services and may include capital gains. If property is not taxed but receives subsidies (e.g. mortgage interest relief and

no VAT) there is a distortional effect towards the purchase of housing. Of course, this may be a government objective.

However, property taxes tend to be regressive, with the taxable value of property often increasing less than proportionately to household income. This particularly disadvantages students, the elderly and single-parent families. Property taxes also do not clearly identify the actual relationship between taxation and spending.

Rates

Rates were a form of property tax. They were a tax on occupation, not ownership and were thus paid by council and private tenants as well as by owner-occupiers. Rebates were used to reduce the regressiveness of the tax, and about one-quarter of households were receiving some level of rebate in 1989.

Rates were cheap to collect, absorbing only 2.5 per cent of the yield, and had most of the other advantages of a property tax..

However, the system became unpopular with the public and the government. Rates were regarded as unfair because a household with many adults received more benefit from local services than did a household with only one adult, but they did not make any greater financial contribution to local government revenue. The government expressed concern about the lack of accountability, since in some areas a large proportion of the electorate were able to vote for higher council spending without having to pay rates, and voters could not easily identify the actual relationship between taxation and spending.

Business rates

The new system of **uniform business rates** came into effect along with the Community Charge in April 1990.

Rates have been retained for businesses but taken out of the control of local authorities. They are now levied by central government at uniform rates for England, Wales and Scotland. The proceeds are then distributed to local authorities on the basis of so much per adult, with extra finance available for those authorities with special problems.

The UBR is based on Inland Revenue rateable valuations and is index-linked to the retail price index (RPI) so that it rises in line with inflation.

The centralization was in part intended to prevent councils from financing additional expenditure through the business rates and also to stop industrial location from being influenced by local rate differences. The ending of local control over the business rate poundage implies that any additional local spending above the amounts received from central government grants and the UBR will be borne fully by house-holders paying local taxation. So the discretionary tax base available to local authorities has been reduced.

Community Charge

The **Community Charge** (often referred to as the 'poll tax') replaced rates in Scotland in 1989 and in England and Wales in 1990. It was a flat rate tax. Some people were exempt, including hospital patients and 18-year-olds still at school. There was some relief for the poorest but most were required to pay a minimum of 20 per cent of the charge. The system of rebates was less generous than with rates, under which system the poorest could receive 100 per cent rebates. The Community Charge was calculated by taking local authority expenditure estimates and deducting central government grant, UBR and other sources of income (e.g. charges for the use of leisure services and council house rents). Then the total was divided by the number of people living in the authority liable to pay the Community Charge. The size varied between authorities depending on the efficiency of the council, the level of service provided, reserves depletion and central government aid.

The Community Charge was introduced with two prime objectives:

- to control local authority expenditure;
- to increase the accountability of local authorities.

If a local authority overspent or used its resources wastefully then it was expected it would suffer in the next local election. This tax's advantages included:

- no disincentive effect since it did not vary with earnings and did not affect the relative prices of different goods and services;
- broadening the base of local taxation so that more of those who consumed local services would share in the cost (it was spread over 40 million people rather than 18 million).

However, local accountability was reduced by the government intervening to cap what they regarded as high-spending local authorities. It also proved to be the most unpopular tax of recent years, contributing to the downfall of Mrs Thatcher as prime minister. Its public unpopularity was due to:

- its perceived unfairness, because it was not based on the ability to pay;
- it making three-quarters of the population worse off;
- the level at which it was set (this in turn was partly the result of the government reducing its funding to local authorities).

Council Tax

The Council Tax came into effect in April 1993. It is a form of property tax with bills determined partly by the value of people's houses and partly by how much each council spends. So, unlike rates, it is determined on the capital value (in effect the sale price) and not the rental value of houses. This is thought to be a more widely understood concept and one easier to estimate. It is based on two adults per home. Additional adults in a household do not pay any extra. There is a discount of 25 per cent for single adults, and a third of the 21 million properties in England and Wales are occupied by just one person. Owners of second homes pay half the full tax on them. Some people on income support receive 100 per cent rebates. So, unlike the rates, there is no minimum contribution.

The tax has lower collection costs than the Community Charge but, like its predecessor, it is a regressive tax. This is because capital values increase less than proportionately to household income and because the top band sets a limit to the tax liability. However, some economists argue that we should not be too concerned about the regressiveness of the Council Tax. This is because it is only one of a number of taxes and what matters most is the incidence of the tax system as a whole rather than a specific part of it. They also claim that local taxation should not deal with redistribution – they see this as the function of central government.

Central government grants

Central government grants to local authorities acknowledge that the tax revenue sources available to local authorities are, on their own, inadequate to support their expenditure.

They also recognise spillover effects – some of the benefits of local expenditure on, for example, education and roads will benefit people outside the area.

The grants also acknowledge that fiscal imbalances may exist, because there is no reason to suppose that the resources and needs of any particular local authority will match. For instance, an area with a high proportion of elderly people will probably have to spend a large amount on social services.

Local taxation remains a controversial area. Economists and politicians are still debating the best tax base, and it is questionable whether it has yet been found.

KEY WORDS

Centralization	Property tax
Decentralization	Rates
Ability to pay principle	Uniform business rates
Benefit principle	Community Charge
Local sales tax	Council Tax
Local income tax	Central government grants

Reading list

Anderton, A., Unit 45 in *Economics*, Causeway Press Ltd., 1991.

Healey, N., and Levačić, R., Chapter 2 in *Supply Side Economics*, 2nd edn, Heinemann Educational, 1992.

O'Hare, M., 'The Council Tax', *Economic Review*, April 1993.

Ridge, M., 'Financing local government from local taxation', *Economics and Business Education Journal*, summer 1993.

Smith, D., Chapter 6 in *Mrs Thatcher's Economics: Her Legacy*, Heinemann Educational, 1992.

Essay topics

1. Explain why taxes are necessary and outline the properties of a good tax. Compare the Community Charge with alternative ways of raising revenue to finance local government. (Joint Matriculation Board, 1991)
2. How should the services currently provided by local authorities be financed? (Associated Examining Board, 1992)
3. Explain why we need taxes and outline the requirements of a good tax. Compare the community charge, the council tax and a local income tax as a means of raising revenue to finance local government. (Northern Examinations and Assessment Board, 1993)

Data Response Question 7

Income tax since 1975

This task is based on a question set by the University of London Examinations and Assessment Council in 1993. Study Table A and answer the questions.

Table A Rates of income tax in three different financial years in the UK

	1975/76		1979/80		1989/90	
	Band of taxable income £	Rate (%)	Band of taxable income £	Rate (%)	Band of taxable income £	Rate (%)
Lower			1–750†	25		
Basic	1–4,500	35	751–10,000	30	1–20,700	25
Higher	4,501–5,000	40	10,001–12,000	40	Over 20,700	40
	5,001–6,000	45	12,001–15,000	45		
	6,001–7,000	50	15,001–20,000	50		
	7,001–8,000	55	20,001–25,000	55		
	8,001–10,000	60	Over 25,000	60		
	10,001–12,000	65				
	12,001–15,000	70				
	15,001–20,000	75				
	Over 20,000	83*				

* Top rate lowered from 83% in 1978/79
† Lowest band of taxable income removed in 1980/81
Source: An *Economic Profile of Britain*, Lloyds Bank plc, 1990

1. Describe the main changes in income tax over the period shown in the table.
2. Would you consider the income tax structure to be more or less progressive in 1979/80 than in 1989/90? Explain your answer.
3. Assume that in 1989/90 every taxpayer had a tax-free allowance of £3000. For a person with a gross income of £30,000, what was (i) the average rate of tax; (ii) the marginal rate of tax?
4. Compare the tax structure existing in 1979/80 with that in 1989/90 in terms of (i) incentives to work; (ii) the distribution of income; (iii) obtaining the highest level of tax revenue.

Chapter Eight

Problems and the future

'Taxation is the most flexible and effective but also a dangerous instrument of social reform.' Gunnar Myrdal

In the 1970s and 80s considerable attention was focused on the problems of fiscal policy. Their existence was one reason for some economists to urge a reduction in the role of **discretionary demand management**. However, whilst problems still exist, and will continue to do so in the future, opinion now seems to be changing, in the 1990s, in favour of a more active role for fiscal policy.

Conflicts in theory
Policy can indeed be constrained by the state of economic knowledge. For fiscal policy, or indeed any other form of government policy, to be fully effective there must be an adequate understanding of how the economy works. Economic policy is designed against the background of a theoretical model. The true model is a subject of considerable controversy. For instance, Keynesians believe that consumption depends on current income, while others (e.g. Milton Friedman) argue that consumption is related to permanent rather than current income. So if the former is true, a change in disposable income as a result of fiscal policy may have a significant impact. However if the latter is true, fiscal policy is likely to be less effective.

The complexity and unpredictability of economic relationships may mean that it is difficult to formulate appropriate economic policies. For instance, it may be difficult to predict the exact size of the **marginal propensity to import** since this will be influenced by a number of factors, such as foreign prices and exchange rates.

Problems of forecasting
A government needs to make forecasts because there is a time delay between the introduction of a policy and its effects. Forecasts need to be as accurate as possible about the direction and extent of changes resulting from policy measures.

The government and a number of groups of economists, including the London Business School, the National Institute of Economic and Social Research (NIESR) and the Cambridge Economic Policy Group

(CEPG), all use **economic models** to explain and forecast the economy. In December 1992 the government appointed a panel of seven independent economists – who have become known as **'the seven wise men'** – to provide an alternative economic forecast to that of the Treasury. These seven include Andrew Britton, director of the NIESR, Professor Wynne Godley of Cambridge University and Professor Patrick Minford of Liverpool University.

Back row: Congdon, Minford, Sentance, Currie Front row: Britton, Davies, Godley

Economic models have had some success in forecasting the behaviour of the economy. However, mistakes can be made in calculating key information and in interpretation. For example, an economist may estimate the multiplier incorrectly or may interpret a fall in private sector spending to be a short-term change which will be self-correcting, whereas it may actually be the start of a recession. The accuracy of forecasts tends to decline the longer the period of time the forecast covers, so it is necessary to design and implement policies quickly.

Time lags

As indicated above, the accuracy of forecasting is important because there is likely to be a **time lag** involved with fiscal policy. One of the key objectives of fiscal policy is stability, with the government trying to avoid large fluctuations in the level of economic activity. In order to achieve this the government may seek to implement a **counter-cyclical**

ECONOMIC FORECASTS

Conventional forecasting relies upon a computer model built from the economist's favourite theory about how the economy works. Using past data, he tries to get the best fit for hundreds of equations that attempt to explain the relation-ships between economic variables. Assumptions about such things as tax rates, which cannot be forecast because they are decided by governments, are then plugged in and the computer cranks out an economic forecast. Economic forecasting will never be 100 % accu-rate, except by luck. But armed with every tool available, an economic forecaster just might earn his keep.

Source: *The Economist*, 13 June 1992

policy. Unfortunately it takes time for a government to assess the eco-nomic situation, to formulate a policy and then implement it. These time lags can be divided into inside and outside lags.

Inside lags

Inside lags arise owing to the time it takes for a government to initiate a policy change. So they occur within the policy-making process. There are two types of inside lags:

- **Recognition lag** (or detection lag) is the time it takes to collect and interpret statistical data.
- **Implementation lag** refers to the time taken to reach a decision on the appropriate policy, to organize the policy instruments and to put them into effect.

Outside lags

Outside lags are concerned with the time it takes for any policy changes to affect the target variables. As with inside lags, there are two forms of outside lags.

- One is the time taken to influence the intermediate policy variables. An example is the time between a tax rate change and its influence on aggregate demand.
- The second form is the time lag between the change in the intermedi-ate policy variable and the target or ultimate policy variables – for instance, the time gap between a change in aggregate demand and the level of employment. This is sometimes referred to as **behav-ioural lag** because it relates to the time it takes for the private sector to adjust to the policy changes.

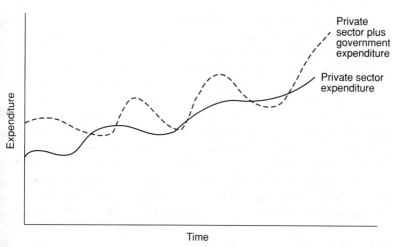

Figure 14 Government policy adding to the economic cycle rather than stabilizing economic activity

Owing to the existence of time lags it is possible for stabilization policy to be destabilizing. It may be the case that it takes two or three years before a stabilization policy fully comes into effect, and by that time the cyclical position of the economy could well have been reversed. Thus the policy may contribute to the cycle rather than act counter-cyclically (see Figure 14). For instance, the tax cuts introduced in the 1988 budget contributed to the existing consumer boom.

Reaction to policy changes

There is the possibility that the economy may not respond as expected to a policy change. For instance, a government may reduce corporation tax with the intention of encouraging investment, but if there is a lack of confidence investment may not rise or may not rise by as much as expected.

Policy changes may themselves influence **expectations.** Households and firms may anticipate the results of changes in economic policy. This reduces the effectiveness of fiscal policy. The problem is how to build expectations into models.

Difficulties of changing government spending and taxation

Fiscal policy would be easier to conduct, and would be more effective, if government expenditure and taxation could be altered more freely. However, much of government expenditure is inflexible, particularly downwards, and changing taxation can be time-consuming. It is difficult, for example, to change salaries to suit the short-run needs of the economy. This is especially true if a government wants to reduce its spending, because cutting salaries would be likely to mean redundancies in public sector employment. These would take time, would be expensive in the short run and would be unpopular.

In addition, much of government expenditure, especially capital expenditure and important social programmes, involves long-term planning. Many government expenditure programmes (for instance road and house building) take a long time to plan and complete. Abandoning a project once it has been started can be extremely wasteful and might not be practicable. (A road cannot be left half built!)

Changing taxes can involve a considerable amount of administrative work. For instance, changes in income tax involve the calculation and distribution of millions of new codes.

Political cycles and pressure groups

Governments tend to relax fiscal policy as general elections approach in order to win support. They also tend to shy away from making politically unpopular decisions. When cuts have to be made in tax privileges or government spending they are often undertaken on the basis of political expediency rather than on the basis of marginal social costs and benefits.

Political influences on fiscal policy also take other forms. Certain groups are more effective at putting pressure on the government. For example, opera companies have been more successful at winning government subsidies than football clubs. So decisions about government spending and tax privileges are influenced by the relative bargaining strengths of different pressure groups.

Policy conflicts

The objectives of a government may conflict. For example, expansionary fiscal policy may help employment and growth but may have an adverse effect on the current account position of the balance of payments and inflation. In the past there has been a conflict between growth and a balance of payments equilibrium. When the UK economy expands, imports tend to be sucked in and, to correct deficits on the current account of the balance of payments, governments engage in deflationary policies. This results in stop/go cycles. This may indicate the need to use a combination of policy measures, for example to combine an expansionary fiscal policy with restrictive monetary policy. Tinbergen argued that a government needs to have at least one policy instrument to achieve each objective.

As we saw in Chapter 3, the three aims of fiscal policy may themselves conflict. A rise in VAT may assist stabilization but may result in a less even distribution of income.

Policy mix

Fiscal policy does not operate in isolation. It is part of a range of policies. A fiscal policy measure may have undesirable effects on other policy measures or may itself be constrained by these. We have seen that if a government follows the rule of linking the growth of the money supply to the growth of GDP, its freedom to engage in discretionary fiscal policy is reduced.

It could be argued that in the past governments have not actively used a sufficient number of policy instruments. In the late 1980s the then Chancellor, Nigel Lawson, relied almost exclusively on changing the rate of interest. As suggested above, demand management cannot achieve all objectives simultaneously and a combination of policy measures need to be used at any one time – for instance, **incomes policy** aimed at inflation and a flexible exchange rate aimed at external balance.

The future of fiscal policy

Although some monetarists are sceptical about the effectiveness and appropriateness of fiscal policy, its importance is currently increasing and seems set to continue to do so. Indeed, possible institutional changes are likely to increase the role of fiscal policy. Independence for the Bank of England and renewed membership of the ERM would take interest rate policy out of the government's hands.

Increased government spending does not have to cause inflation and balance of payments problems. Capital spending involving construction can have a significant impact on the domestic economy without sucking in imports. Only some 7 per cent of the spending on construction is subsequently spent on imports. Construction and civil engineering currently have vast unused capacity and so transport infrastructure can be improved relatively cheaply and without creating inflationary pressure.

A fiscal expansion that is targeted closely on the long-term unemployed should have smaller inflationary consequences than one that affects the short-term unemployment.

Nevertheless, fiscal policy will have to be used carefully. It is important that measures used to increase aggregate demand should be accompanied by measures which will promote aggregate supply. In the past there have been occasions when one side has been neglected with adverse consequences for employment and inflation. So the policy mix has to be right with, for instance, expansionary fiscal policy accompanied by supply side measures to improve the workings of the labour market (e.g. promotion of training).

Inside and outside time lags should be reduced whilst a longer-term perspective is taken on public sector spending plans. Some major problems still remain to be solved, including our poor international trade performance and lack of economic growth. Fiscal policy has a role to play in solving these and achieving steady and sustainable growth.

The quotation at the start of this chapter states that taxation is, potentially, a flexible and powerful instrument in improving welfare. Whilst there are limits to the flexibility of both taxation and public spending, there is still a high degree of possible adjustment. Fiscal policy is likely to continue to be an important form of government policy and to have a significant impact on our lives.

KEY WORDS

Discretionary demand management	Recognition lag
Marginal propensity to import	Implementation lag
Economic models	Outside lags
Seven wise men	Behavioural lag
Time lag	Expectations
Counter-cyclical policy	Policy mix
Inside lags	Incomes policy

Index